ACKNOWLEDGEMENTS

I want to acknowledge all the people who "wrote" the story that I told in this book...

Pauline Ledeen the original Jewish Jail Lady, Gateways Hospital and the Jewish Committee for Personal Service, the Beit T'Shuvah Board of Directors and Donors and all the people who a part of the Beit T'Shuvah community.

I thank Reeva Hunter Mandelbaum—friend, editor, maestro—for sustaining her vision of *Sacred Housekeeping* and restoring mine when I gave up. Reeva ploughed through twenty years of my writings and envisioned this book.

John Sullivan who created the book design and made it his personal mission to make it happen.

Fanya Cohen for believing in and carrying the message.

Susan Reneau for translating my script and loose-leaf papers into type.

Donald Freed for encouraging me to write.

All the people who have believed in me and in Beit T'Shuvah.

PRAISE FOR SACRED HOUSEKEEPING

"With her inspirational blend of Jewish wisdom, Torah Spirituality, 12-Step practice, personal experience, outrageous wit, and just plain common sense Harriet Rossetto's "*Sacred Housekeeping*" has set a new standard for personal integrity and authenticity in the professional recovery literature.

Speaking from her heart, soul and brain at the same time, Harriet harmoniously integrates thought and action, emotion and intellect —without neglecting one for the other. Pointing out that the "good parts and bad parts" of our identity are umbilically connected, Harriet challenges us to find the courage, faith and honesty to cherish BOTH as essential and divine components of our humanity, and to implement this critical task by exercising accountability and responsibility on a daily basis.

Please read this funny, sad, simple but profound book! Everyone, not just alcoholics, other addicts, and co-dependent persons - in or out of recovery - will find that Harriet's message will help to protect and preserve their sanity, safety and self-esteem, and in certain instances may change or even save their lives. At least, that's what it did for me when I read it in a single sitting one rainy afternoon."

–GARRETT O'CONNOR, MD, Associate Clinical Professor of Psychiatry, UCLA, Chief Psychiatrist, Betty Ford Center (2003-2007), President, Betty Ford Instute (2008-2011)

"I have read your book in one sitting. I couldn't put it down. Not only is it full of riches, guides to a spiritual life and frank and vivid truths, it is also wonderfully written and well paced. The power of what you offer is undeniable. I was moved to tears and laughter several times. Thank you."

–LEONARD NIMOY, World Renowned Film & Television Actor

"*Sacred Housekeeping* is a tour de force of courage, determination, and the kind of potent, tenacious goodness that surely changes the world. It's about recovering from addiction but it's also about recovering our souls. Harriet Rossetto is a cultural icon, a woman who I think of to gain strength. She's a talented, brave, honest writer with an edgy, irreverent sense of humor that blasts apart stereotypes to touch the truth. Highly recommend this book!"

–JUDITH ORLOFF, MD, *New York Times* Bestselling Author, *Emotional Freedom*

"*Sacred Housekeeping* is Harriet Rossetto's honest, enlightening and amusing look at her life before and during Beit T'Shuvah, a rehab clinic/ halfway house/ synagogue she founded, dedicated to the idea that no one is beyond redemption."

–ROBERTO LOIDERMAN, *The Jewish Journal of Greater Los Angeles*

"I literally could not put [*Sacred Housekeeping*] down. I was engaged, moved, challenged and enlightened […] it is a delightful revelation of the human condition. I would tell everyone I know to read this book."

–RABBI LAURA OWENS, Member of The Southern California Board of Rabbi's

"Honest Gritty and inspired/inspiring."

–DR BILL RESNICK, Chairman of the Beit T'Shuvah Board of Directors

SACRED
HOUSEKEEPING
a spiritual memoir

HARRIET ROSSETTO

AuthorHouse™
1663 Liberty Drive
Bloomington, IN 47403
www.authorhouse.com
Phone: 1-800-839-8640

Cover & book design by John Sullivan
Cartoon by Cuyler Black
Edited by Reeva Hunter Mandelbaum

For information regarding permission,
call 310-204-5200 or contact us at our website:
www.sacredhousekeeping.com or write to:
Harriet Rossetto
8831 Venice Blvd.
Los Angeles, California 90034

Published by AuthorHouse   03/01/2013

ISBN: 978-1-4772-9551-9 (sc)
ISBN: 978-1-4772-9550-2 (e)

Library of Congress Control Number: 2012922723

*I dedicate this book to my
Partner-in-Redemption,
Mark Jay Borovitz.
You are a fierce prophet.*

SACRED HOUSEKEEPING
a spiritual memoir

FOREWORD

I met Harriet Rossetto for the first time in 1984 when I was sitting in prison in Chino, California, waiting to celebrate one of the Jewish holidays. I was able to see my first wife, daughter and step-daughter, so I did not pay much attention to her. She was part of the group of Jewish jail workers from Los Angeles that were trying to help people incarcerated not reoffend. Since I knew that my incarceration was a mistake, I was sure I didn't need their help! The next time I met Harriet was in 1987, again in prison in Chino, California. We butted heads on what Jewish criminals needed when they got out. She was/is a Social Worker and I was an inmate, but of course I knew better!

We started a conversation that has lasted 25 years and is growing and going stronger now than it did then.

Harriet is an amazing woman. She has taken so many thousands of people by the hand and led them to their rightful place in the world and these people in turn, have done the same with thousands of others. Harriet's story, her teachings, her wisdom and wit are contained in this book, and she will lead you by the hand to a life of passion, purpose, meaning and joy! I know this to be true because I am one of the thousands who has found all of these and more by being Harriet's student, devotee, partner, Rabbi and, oh yeah, her husband! Thanks Harr, for being you and teaching all of us to be who we are!

Rabbi Mark Borovitz

PREFACE

When I was 45—financially ruined, heart-broken (again), and at rock bottom—I experienced the miracle that changed my life.

I was not a person who believed in miracles back then. But one came anyway—in the form of a tiny *Los Angeles Times* classified ad for a Social Worker, "a person of Jewish background and culture to help incarcerated Jewish offenders. MSW required." That job led me to my life's work as founder and CEO of Beit T'Shuvah, and to my husband and partner-in-the-mission, Rabbi Mark Borovitz, an ex-con.

For over 20 years, Beit T'Shuvah and I have grown up together. In learning how to heal and nourish broken souls, I have healed my own. This book, *Sacred Housekeeping*, is about my journey, and the lessons and spiritual insights I learned along the way, and how Beit T'Shuvah and our treatment model developed. It's not a textbook. I am not a Jewish scholar, and take full credit for the ways I've both illuminated and mangled Jewish teachings. It is my story and an attempt to answer and analyze the core question I am often asked about what we do: how is transformation of the human spirit possible?

In the early days, I was visiting Jewish felons from Chino to Sybil Brand, Tehachapi to Terminal Island and more. I sat across the glass from good people who did bad things; those who knew right, and compulsively did wrong; well-intentioned people who stole hearts and swindled souls.

Some of my clients were parents and grandparents, attorneys and teachers with backgrounds and histories similar to mine. I would drive the backroads home and wonder how they got there—not just in lock down, but there, in that place, in their lives. I began to see myself in them. Not because I had done what they had done, or been arrested, or had ever been addicted to drugs or alcohol, but because I was also out of control and living a double life.

I was a professional with a Master's Degree, a PTA mom who made cupcakes, and made a mess everywhere else. I wouldn't pay my bills until the mailbox exploded with pink envelopes. I was a parking-ticket scofflaw, and lost many library cards for failure to return books. I burned up a car engine for lack of oil after putting off maintenance for months. My belongings and surroundings were trashed. My desk harbored piles of unfinished projects that would have saved the world. My relationships, of course, were as erratic and unkempt—and at times, dangerous--as anything else. I embodied the habits of highly ineffective people!

Beit T'Shuvah started when I received a grant to offer transitional living to a few recently-released Jewish felons in an old house in downtown LA. More than 20 years later, it's a thriving community with three buildings in West Los Angeles, an $8 million + budget, cutting-edge programs, engaged philanthropic support. It's for the healing of addictions, self-destructive behaviors, and people whose lives have become—like mine was—unmanageable. The Integrative Recovery Model at Beit T'Shuvah, is a unique blend of Jewish spirituality, cognitive behavioral therapy, 12-step philosophy and the creative arts. We are also an urban kibbutz where soul work sustains the community, where the goal is to uncover your soul and re-cover connection, where you get to know who you are and what you have to contribute and provided opportunities to do what you do best. It is a place that heals the healers.

Beit T'Shuvah is very personal too. It has allowed me to love my work and work with my love. It's a reflection of Mark and me, and our individual and marital spiritual growth. We teach what we have learned and live our struggles and our spiritual victories out loud for all to see. In the process we heal others who turn around and heal others, while we all heal ourselves. I am blessed. We are blessed and we bless others.

I have witnessed many miraculous transformations. I have learned there is no secret, no one way to wholeness (holiness). I believe that as human beings we are holy, and part of a Divine Plan; that faith works and change happens. It starts with small, do-able things—making your bed, uncluttering your closets, sticking to a routine. It's honoring commitments to yourself and others. It's understanding that everything we need to live at peace requires daily maintenance: body, soul, thoughts and emotions, relationships, living space and the stuff of daily survival. It is acting in kind or loving ways no matter what you feel. It's believing change is possible—and mandatory—and that redemption happens. God is truly in the up-keep.

Epiphanies and peak moments evaporate quickly, leaving the messes and clutter of daily life: the garbage, the laundry, the bills, the constant need to replenish the refrigerator, wardrobe, gas tank, bank account. Maintenance has no rush, no payoff, no applause, no end. It can be—frankly—boring. Its rewards are internal. It is a statement to yourself that you matter, that caring for yourself honors God. It is a sacred obligation.

Sacred Housekeeping is my attempt to define events that led to Beit T'Shuvah, the spiritual insights that Beit T'Shuvah is built upon, and how it operates in action. I have attempted to identify the ah-ha's, the light bulbs that lit my way from lost to found, from half-heartedness and holes, to wholeness and holiness.

Redemption is my addiction and my mission. It is my faith, passion and my purpose.   I carry it to all who still suffer in silence.

Harriet Rossetto, LCSW
CEO and Founder of Beit T'Shuvah
Los Angeles, California 90034

EXPECT A MIRACLE

I hit bottom in Laguna Nigel in 1983.

I was in my 40's, a former social worker, a missionary in search of a mission, unable to find my purpose or place in the world. I was jobless, penniless, homeless and hopeless. My only child just left for college, and took with her my raison d'être. I found comfort in food and looked for love in all the wrong places. I was out of shape in all my affairs, and addicted to despair.

My entire life I'd changed husbands, costumes, hair styles, ideologies—desperately seeking an identity that would make me whole. In my romantic moments, I had grandiose visions of saving the world. In my darkest moments of self-loathing, I hid in bed and gave up on life. I was literally strung out between the extremes of possibility and hopelessness. One part of me would have a vision, fall in love with a guru, an idea or a Prince Charming; the other would quit at the first obstacle or fall out of love as quickly as I fell in. The missionary zeal to make a difference in the world was squelched by my inner sloth.

This latest idiocy left me broke, with nowhere to go.

I came of age pre-Women's Movement. According to my mother at that time, I was sent to college to find a husband and to prepare myself for a—God-forbid—career, which meant, a way to support myself if he should die. My choice of husband was doctor or lawyer; my choice of career was teacher or social worker. She preferred lawyers: "Doctors keep terrible hours and are more likely to fool around."

I got into Tufts, married the requisite Harvard Jewish Law School graduate. He was a Democrat and liked classical music—my only requirements. I was gifted with all linens, china and crystal necessary to live happily ever after. I spent my wedding night at the Plaza Hotel in New York City on the way to a honeymoon in Niagara Falls.

As soon as the sun came up, I called my mother and begged to come home.

"It's bridal jitters; it'll get better."

It didn't.

I moved with my new husband, "the catch," to Minneapolis, to be a housewife. And while he clerked for a Minnesota Supreme Court Justice, I ran wild—really wild. My rebellion had begun.

By day I was a college English major, seducing my professors, chasing the meaning of life; by night I was a good-girl wife. I learned to cook and "set a fine table" with the good stuff. I used the monogrammed tablecloth once and left it crumpled and crumby on the floor of the closet until we divorced. The "R" monogrammed towels worked with the next husband.

I married again and had a child. One part of me was über-mom— the right everything (parenting books, toys, schools, friends, etc).

The other part of me hated the responsibility of motherhood, smoked dope while my daughter napped and carried on an affair with the elevator man in our Westside apartment. I divorced a second time, and moved the elevator man in. When I tired of him, he extorted my mother and stepfather at gunpoint, threatening to harm my daughter if they didn't hand over $5,000. When he got out of prison he terrorized me.

I moved 3000 miles away to Los Angeles to try to escape and also figure out how this happened. How had an intelligent woman from a nice Jewish family, with a master's degree in social work ended up running down 72nd Street in the middle of the night being chased by her ex-lover wielding a broken beer bottle and screaming, "I'll run you out of New York, bitch."

My mother stared at me as I packed, and quietly asked: "Harriet, where were your instincts?"

Ironically, the relationship that caused me to hit bottom when I was in Laguna Niguel wasn't even romantic. I had followed Al, a pied piper who seduced me with flattery and the promise of being a "business partner" in real estate seminars that sold blue-sky to dreamers, and convinced me to apply my skills to getting people to give him their money. "You're too old to be a hippie," he said.

Al taught me how to sell sizzle, rape homes of their equity, and cheat the legal system of judgments against him. He was giving everybody the finger and I applauded him as a Robin Hood until he did it to me. When the money started flowing in, he bought his bitchy girlfriend a big diamond and kicked me to the curb.

~

I'm desperate. I call my friend Peggy. I'd once rejected her 'Science of Mind, power of positive thinking' and metaphysical beliefs. It's hard to admit, but I admire and envy her spirit. Because of the seminars, I've been reading self-help and success literature. Peggy and a lot of people are going to see a woman who talks about miracles and can make your dreams come true. I'm not in the business of miracles or spirituality in any form, so I think it's bullshit.

Peggy sees that I'm in a bad place. I confess how bad, what's going on, that I feel I have no reason to live. I ask for help. She hands me a business card: "Call Janet before you check out. Maybe she can help you."

I look at it:

Expect a Miracle.
Janet Levy, Science of Mind Practitioner

She has a Jewish last name, but works in a church. It's weird to me. Curiosity overtakes cynicism and I make an appointment. She's short, round and warm, nice eyes, a version of the good mother I hadn't had or been.

She hugs me. "What is it you want, dear? Why are you here?"

"That's the problem, I don't know. When I get what I think I want, I don't want it any more or it doesn't want me. What I want is to know what I want."

"Do you pray?"

"You must be kidding! I'm Jewish. I'm an intellectual. We don't pray!"

"Then I'll pray for you," she offers. "Close your eyes and take my hand." I do.

"Father of the Universe, take this woman by the hand and guide her to her rightful work.   She knows she has a mission but she doesn't know what it is."

We open our eyes and look at one another.

"That's it?"

"That's it for now. You just pay attention."

I don't want to offend her, but I don't feel any different. In fact, I'm self-conscious and leave furtively, looking up and down the street to make sure no one I know sees me coming out of a church.   I felt like a traitor to all the "isms" that counted on me to believe in them: Judaism, atheism, existentialism, anarchism, my father's long-ago socialism.

A few days later, I'm still miracle-less, jobless, with $64.00 in the bank.   I need to find work. I get the paper, and glance through the classifieds.

And I see it.

IT.

FINDING PURPOSE

Nothing in Sales & Marketing seemed right, and I was about to toss the paper in the recycling bin. I'd gotten bored with social worker jobs. The money was nothing. That's when I met Al. But I heard the still, small voice: see what Social Work has to offer. If I hadn't been paying attention, I might've ignored it. Instead, I turned to the last page and scanned down to the smallest ad on the bottom:

Person of Jewish background and culture
to work with Jewish criminal offenders.
MSW required.

Jewish outlaws…?

The words escaped without my permission: "My God, this shit works…"

The hairs on my arms stood up. My body tingled. A lady prays for me to be guided to my rightful work and three days later a job with my name on it pops up? On the outside I was a nice Jewish girl with intellectual pretensions, but my hidden identity was a Madam or Gun Moll. I kept my inner outlaw under wraps most of my life, ashamed of my attraction to bad boys and True Crime. I didn't even know there were Jewish criminals, let alone a career helping them. Maybe I could even find one to take home. I couldn't wait to tell my mother, who thought all Jewish boys were doctors, lawyers or accountants!

~

I had been a missionary child searching for a mission; my heroines were Eleanor Roosevelt, Emma Goldman and Dorothy Day. My high school yearbook predicted I would save the world. Deep down I couldn't shake my desire to save people. Even back in New York I'd worked at a kind of halfway house for people coming out of state mental hospitals. I would take them shopping and try to teach them how to live on their own. It was as if everything I'd done and been—wrong and right—led me to this moment.

The moment of ah-ha is a jolt, a challenge to how we view the world and the feelings and choices emanating from that worldview. The metaphors of all religions and spiritualities apply: out of the cave into the light; I was blind and now I see; asleep now awake; Jacob wrestles with the angel and becomes Israel. Born again.

My negative, who-gives-a-shit belief system instantly shattered, and I made the rational decision to have faith. I didn't think of the miracle I was asked to expect in a woo-woo, mystical sense (and probably still don't), but I understood if I defined what happened as pure luck or coincidence, nothing much would change. Seen as Divine Guidance, everything would change. No burning bush or lightning bolt, but it was my spiritual awakening. And that moment is how I see the Genesis story of Beit T'Shuvah and of bringing me toward meeting Mark. That decision made all the difference, and it changed my trajectory.

I wonder if the still, small voice that told me to turn to the social work section, was part of a Divine Plan already in motion, leading me to my true purpose. Had opening myself to prayer, to something different and better, prepared my heart and soul to get me to where I was meant to be?

Expect a miracle.

This much I knew for sure: I'd finally found my little corner of the world to repair.

HERE I AM

I joined a band of quixotic social workers, hidden from view in the basement of a mental hospital, and became known as The Jewish Jail Lady. We were led by Pauline Ledeen, a woman in her eighties, who'd been visiting Jews in jail for 50 years. The inmates called her "Bubbe" Theresa. For years Pauline trekked to county, state and federal jails and prisons in Southern California, ferreting out the Jewish inmates, bringing them gifts at Chanukah, boxes of Matzos and Seders at Passover and prayer books and New Year's Cards for Rosh Hashanah. They were the forgotten Jews. She wanted them to know they weren't forgotten by the outside, and that there would be a place for them to return to. Our slogan was: Serving Jews who are Serving Time.

Pauline was an attorney, but left her law practice because she felt it was wrong to refuse help to those who couldn't pay. I confessed to her that I had always thought (and been taught) that the reason I couldn't ask for money was because I had no self-esteem.

"There's nothing wrong with you," she assured. "You're a Jew!"

I didn't realize it then, but this stubborn belief would become the basic foundation of the Beit T'Shuvah business plan: no one in need is refused for the inability to pay. I still don't feel it's kosher to profit from people's misery or take financial advantage of their vulnerability. As a matter of fact, the Torah has more laws governing kosher money than kosher food. The Torah tells us that if we do what is right, with good intention, God will provide. My interpretation of this has been that if we reached out to people at their most vulnerable and helped them to become the people they were intended to be, then their collective gratitude and desire to give to others what they had been given would sustain and grow our mission.

I was hooked, eager to get to jail every morning.

The stories were better than anything I had read: the self-effacing Talmudic scholar who shot his ex-wife in front of their children when he couldn't meet her increasing demands for higher alimony; a Rabbi arrested for "vashing the money" to build a religious school, and on and on.

I went to court on behalf of an actor in Beverly Hills who'd been high on cocaine and booze and worried about his bills, and got arrested for passing a note to the bartender where he was drinking: "I need $500 for my rent—blink or I'll shoot!" He flubbed the line: "don't blink or I'll shoot." The sentencing judge laughed out loud when he read my notes recommending treatment: "This is a Woody Allen movie," he said.

But what wasn't funny is that I began to see that my clients' lives had gone sideways, spun irrevocably, hellishly out of control. What they did or where they lived or what they had didn't matter. They ran the gamut—from tycoons, doctors, lawyers, teachers, grandmas, shrinks, Rabbis, and musicians, to gangsters, cons, and bums. There was one common denominator: addiction—to alcohol, drugs, gambling, sex and love, shopping, shoplifting and a peculiarly Jewish one I named compulsive Macherism (people who spend money they don't have, to buy things they don't need, to impress people they don't like).

~

It's my first week on the job.

The extremes of the people I work with unleash extreme emotions in me. I love them and despise them. Feel compassion and disgust. I believe them, though I know they're lying. They have glorious intentions, heinous actions. They charmingly bite the hands of those who feed them, break the hearts of those who love them, and rape the souls of those who trust them.

I arrive at Sybil Brand County Jail for Women, with my safe identification card around my neck, ensuring I can leave. I sit at my place, in pressed slacks and pumps, carrying a briefcase. Jane checks me out from the other side of the double-pane glass, in orange state-issued jumpsuit and handcuffs. I learn she's my age, a graduate of Hunter College in New York, a high school English teacher, her daughter is the exact same age as mine. Jane's addiction to heroin started after her husband returned from Vietnam with a habit, and eventually she started dealing to support his and her growing habits.

Shards of myself show up everywhere, in every story I hear. Lovesick women who've followed boyfriends into drugs, crime or worse. Women who abandoned their children for crack or slot machines. A grandmother who scammed a bank out of $300,000 to buy Ronald Reagan's house—so she could be something more than she was to those she loved. "I wanted to leave it for my grandchildren," she says, like it still makes sense to her on some level.

I pay taxes, have good credit, a master's degree. I function. I haven't shot heroin or sold it, but I've messed around with plenty of recreational drugs, and hung out with bad men who sold them. I'd flirted with some pretty dark stuff. I never thought out the consequence that I could go to jail for smoking pot or dropping acid. In my mind, I was rebelling, not committing a crime!

For the next few weeks I can't avoid thinking about how close to the edge I have been, more than once. 'There but for the grace of God...' is a refrain I hear again and again as I drive the unfamiliar freeways home from Tehachapi or Lancaster or Chino. They are no longer just words.

And I think about Jane.

She is me. The only difference is that I wasn't caught, and that—for now—I had the façade together and was able to pass.

She's my lesson.

~

For most of us, the outer pieces are in order, properly arranged on the mantelpieces of our lives, while the inner might be cracking. My jail addicts couldn't keep the secret. The outside was cracking, and they stopped trying, said "fuck it," and broke down publicly, smashing the code of silence. I began to see them all symbolically, that they were carrying the message that the whole system is broken, forcing the rest of us out of denial, sending us back to the instruction manual on How to Be Human.

Addiction is a progressive disease. Eventually you do things you know you would never do. What begins as a solution to a problem, becomes the problem. Just as Jane never anticipated ending up in a jail cell, I never predicted that my search for the perfect bad boy would end with me running up 72nd Street in New York in the middle of the night being chased by my latest love waving a broken beer bottle at me, threatening to "run my ass out of New York," or sitting in a hospital emergency room in a wheel chair marked "Transfer to Bellevue" after a semi-suicide attempt. I thought I was in love and it turned me on to see the pistol peeking out of his jacket. I never connected it with real violence or crime: it was sexy.

Jane and all my other clients were battling the world, hidden from themselves. But I was battling myself, hidden from the world. I knew I was changing in some big and important way.

But what I didn't know is that the unfolding miracle had not yet fully realized.

It was Chanukah at Chino and we were standing in line—Pauline and the five irreverent do-gooders humming Dreidle, Dreidle, Dreidle…. We had latkes and gift-wrapped socks for our inmates, and squeezed inside with mothers, wives, kids. A blond woman carried a big aluminum foil tin of kugel. She introduced herself, "I'm Jewish by injection." I noticed her husband. He was huge—shaved head, mean looking. A tough guy. Not a miracle or soulmate material, not even somebody I wanted to know. But I did remember him when we met again a few years later.

For now, I had heard the call and answered *Hineni*—Hebrew for here I am.

EITHER/OR TO BOTH/AND

I struggled with love/hate emotions toward my clients. Some days were really tough.

Like when an orthodox man, President of his Shul, was arrested after his 6-year old daughter was diagnosed with gonorrhea—"we were just cuddling and her nightgown must have ridden up," he explained.

I, like most, took for granted that the normal response to the child molester and someone who commits atrocious acts is that he is a soul-less monster. But the contrasts and contradictions provoked a spiritual reaction in me. Instead of becoming more jaded and judgmental, I found myself becoming more empathic, asking introspective questions.

Did addicts and criminals not have a soul—or was it broken?

Could I find a soul inside someone who seemed soul-less and whose actions were treacherous?

And if that soul existed and was broken, could it be mended?

I began to see myself in all my clients, not just Jane. Maybe not myself exactly, but that beneath the surface, the human condition part, the spiritual part was similar. Their extremes were more extreme and the things they did to escape or soothe themselves were worse than what I had done, but I sensed that the line between "them" and "us" was an illusion.

Didn't I have my own incongruities and ambiguities? My own lapses?

Didn't I alternate between extremes?

Didn't I have a dark side?

Every day in my mission, I felt like I was fighting a holy war—struggling to balance the good and evil I was witnessing, working hard to understand and heal my own broken-ness so I could mirror wholeness back to the divided souls behind the glass. This much I knew— I wasn't going to heal anyone else if I couldn't heal myself and make peace with my own extremes, incongruities and dark impulses as well. And, I was finding my soul working with people who appear to be soul-less.

It necessitated a paradigm shift.

I read all the relationship and co-dependency books, listened to countless tapes, signed up for lots of self-help seminars, flirted with Eastern mysticism, meditation and yoga, kept journals and mostly avoided romantic relationships.

Epiphanies quickly evaporate; realizations don't bring results. I had to find a path to wholeness that I could follow. For me, there was no quick fix, one-size-fits-all answer. My search took me to metaphysics, Twelve Steps, Jungian shadow work, Buddhist psychology and Jewish wisdom. Luckily, my journey as Jewish Jail Lady coincided with the Recovery Movement blossoming in Los Angeles. It was a new way of integrating spirituality and psychology, defining addiction as a dis-ease of body, mind and spirit, and requiring the treatment that integrated psychology and spirituality.

I learned that Carl Jung helped Bill Wilson draft the 12 Steps, and was relieved: If Jung believed God could help tormented people, maybe there was something to this. Scott Peck, a psychiatrist, wrote *The Road Less Traveled* and talked about spirituality. John Bradshaw became the face of the recovery movement for therapists, conferring credibility on the 12 Step, AA Path to recovery. Co-dependency became a household word. At meetings and workshops, the inner-children came out to play. The Jewish response was Jewish renewal, mysticism and meditation. Jews who had left Judaism to find spirituality in Buddhism were named JUBUS.

One text in a book of Jewish wisdom gave me a template of how to make sense of what I was experiencing:

A great Rabbi's disciples asked him how could he so readily understand the problems of gamblers and thieves and other troubled men and women who came from the darker places of life. The rabbi explained:

> *When they come I listen hard to them. I look deep into their eyes and I discover that their weaknesses are reflections of my own. It is not that I have done what they have done but I sense within me their lusts, desires, weaknesses, temptation. I find in them, myself... Once there was a man who came to me with confessions of his transgressions and though I listened attentively I could find nothing whatsoever*

that I had in common with him. There was nothing of his sins that were in me. Then I knew the truth: I must be hiding something within myself of which I was not fully conscious.

I fell in love with this teaching. It was an answer to the riddle of good and evil: we are equally endowed with the potential for good or evil, no "us" and "them." We are all BOTH. When I couldn't see the common ground or contain the disparities, I knew I hadn't looked deep enough: what is in you is in me!

This wisdom ultimately defined my mission. It felt prophetic, and it was though I had been appointed or anointed not only to help my clients, but to carry this message to the Jews on the outside.

Starting with myself.

~

When I was a married college student finishing my degree in Minnesota, I got a job working in a field position with the Girl Scouts of America—overseeing sales of short bread and Thin Mints, organizing den mothers for camping trips. The irony is not lost on me even now: by day, I was a real Girl Scout, green uniform and everything; at night, I was out of control—naked and drunk, sleeping with the poet John Berryman, my Humanities 54 Professor. I thought my double life made me special and unique.

Girl Scout and Wild Girl. Marjorie Morningstar and Shirley Morgenstern.

Even though the schism of these two impulses tore me apart (as all the other schisms in me did), I knew that I not only liked both, I WAS both. I wanted my husband—the safe bet, the smart lawyer, the nice kid who went to temple and worshipped his parents. And I also wanted the bad boy, the tough kid—the edge. But I didn't understand that there was anything but either/or.

I'd always careened between the opposing forces within me: convention and rebellion; the person I was supposed to be and the defiant one. One was lazy and the other ambitious; one read Dostoyevsky, the other sneaked peeks at *The National Enquirer*; one listened to Bach, the other to Billie Holiday; one was a New York foodie, the other slunk surreptitiously into McDonald's; one wanted to save the world and the other wanted to stay in bed.

~

Like my clients, I had all of the characteristics of addiction and compulsiveness when it came to a lot of things, including but not limited to: men, paperwork and procrastination, and the big one—food.

I was also addicted to despair, not to drugs. Drugs take you out of your misery. Misery was my high. It defined me. It was my consolation prize for not being pretty enough or thin enough or popular enough. Hopelessness sedated my spirit, relieving me of self-loathing and the need to pursue my dreams. Who was I kidding?

And I was addicted to unfinished-ness—a thousand grand ideas that lead to abandoned missions. My life was a string of starts powered by grandiose, illogical thoughts. I never completed anything. When it got difficult, I quit. Instant gratification wasn't soon enough. No self-discipline.

But the big one was food: my deepest, darkest lurking shadow and secret.

I was a fat, klutzy kid who wet the bed, the last one picked for any team. Food had always been my best friend and worst enemy. All I ever wanted was to be able to eat whenever and whatever I wanted and be a perfect size 6. I was laughed at undressing in the locker room. I sneaked and hoarded snacks, bought every magic potion, starved myself, stuffed myself, hated myself. I was either fat or thin. I threw cookies or cakes away and retrieved them from the garbage in the middle of the night. I snuck out to McDonald's for Big Macs and lied to my friends. I ate alone, after dark when no one could see me, as if then the calories didn't count.

Almost every girl/woman who comes to Beit T'Shuvah for drug addiction has a secondary eating disorder. More and more it is emerging as a secret primary disorder. They binge, purge and restrict, obsessing unremittingly about weight and body image. They compete with one another for the gold medals of sickest, skinniest, most frequent purger. Their moods are determined by the scale and the mirror. Their goal is size -0. "Look at me. I'm invisible." Their worst curse is "fat pig."

I didn't binge or purge, but I obsessed.

I bought every book or shake that promised miracles, tried every diet. I grew up pre-purge; we didn't know about anorexia or bulimia. My solution was half and half—stuff or starve—usually seasonally determined. The threat of bathing suit and the number 200 kept me in check. I suffered a serious mood disorder—the scale determined my mood. As with all addicts, if I didn't like what I felt, I craved the comfort of carbs and fat, hating myself with every bite.

Monday I'll go on a diet, I swear.

Just one.

When getting to a size 6 didn't fix it, I became a size 14 and wore caftans. I obsessed and agonized about my body and appearance no matter my size. I also lied to myself that what I looked like didn't matter. My behavior told a different story. The rituals of eating and dieting, shopping and costuming myself occupied at least half of my time, thoughts and activities.

The easiest diet I found was falling in love and that worked from high school through college. During the up phase, I literally lost my appetite, usually for a couple of months. Neuroscientists are now studying new love, the biology of desire, and describe the chemicals that are released as equivalent to a speed bath. The chemicals are time-released and when the love phase is over you crash hard. The only comfort for lost love is found food and the compulsive cycle starts over until a new love is found.

In desperation I had tried Overeaters Anonymous and read in the pamphlet: "The only people for whom this program will not work are people whose psychological survival depends on a sense of their own uniqueness." I was contemptuous of people with group solutions, particularly if they involved God. I stayed for awhile, but wouldn't let them mess with "my uniqueness." I showed them, of course, quit and gained another 10 pounds.

But as powerful as my contempt was, my hatred of hypocrisy—even in myself— wouldn't allow me to preach something I couldn't practice. One day after leaving Jail, I decided to stop in at an OA meeting, my first one in a long time.

Refracted through the lens of my new mission and growing familiarity with addiction, I sat in the meetings and listened—for real this time. I heard a different message that re-defined my personal struggle. I heard that what I had been feeding was a spiritual hunger; I had been feeding my body but my soul was starving. No amount of food would fill that hole. Food was simply fuel, the body a home for the soul. It was to be nurtured and nourished, not abused and despised.

I was still in a tug-of-war with myself, no one winning. I was still a junk-food junkie in the truest sense. I still became distraught when the scale changed, and all the issues I knew I had. But something was changing—not on the outside so much, but inside, in how I felt about myself.

I began to see that the problem was not even a problem. It was the core of the human condition: the drive for perfection. I started to reshape my perception of addiction and criminal behaviors as a spiritual as well as a psychological condition. Most therapies attempt to apply an outside solution to an internal problem; to treat a soul-sickness with material band-aids, believing that fixing the outsides would heal the insides. This self-deception causes the "hole in the soul," the gap between inside and outside that drives us to fill up with pride or food or stuff or substances, endlessly seeking, never satisfied. It is the condition that AA defines as "one is too many and a thousand is never enough."

I remember the ah-ah moment when I merged, comfortable in the both/and space of ambiguity. I could listen to Mozart and Frank Sinatra. I could like nice boys and bad boys, good literature and "Chick-lit," the High Road and the Gutter, *National Enquirer* and *New York Times*. All of it was the real me, my own kaleidoscope of different colored bits and pieces constantly rearranging themselves to allow my authenticity. I was free at last!

Girl Scout and Wild Girl.

I had started my journey from either/or to both/and.

T'SHUVAH

In the early days, we brought Jewish Holidays to the inmates by attending the jail Seders, Chanukah gatherings, and High Holiday services. In sad rooms behind barbed wire and steel, my outdated view of Judaism as a collection of irrelevant rules and rituals was corrected, my vision deepened.

I couldn't know it then, but one-by-one, the building blocks of Beit T'Shuvah's integrative approach were being put in place. I began to see that Judaism and psychology, although different, confronted the same paradoxes and profound questions of human existence.

At my first state prison Seder, the Rabbi explained that *Mitzrayim*, the word for Egypt, literally means narrow places. We are commanded to examine our own narrow places, and to see the story symbolically, for the Pharaohs and enslavements and stuck-ness within us that we impose upon ourselves.

I had been to many Seders in my life before that one. They were family occasions to endure—"Thanksgiving with matzos"—as Rabbi Omer-Man used to say. The Haggadah was a long and boring story about our ancestors getting out of slavery that we had to read out loud so we could eat. It seemed irrelevant and never occurred to me—or anyone I knew—that the Passover story was more than historical, that it was a metaphor for something important and meaningful. But now I was interested, and every word coming out of the Rabbi's mouth was like a revelation.

Freedom is a process—getting out of external bondage is liberty, but not yet freedom.

In liberty we shake off the shackles imposed by others but until we develop an inner authority, we are not free.

We are slaves to our impulses, appetites, and life-destroying thoughts and habits.

The Power greater than ourselves that we need to recover is an internalized Power, the exercise of the free will that makes us human.

There is no freedom without self-discipline!

We can only be free when Moses and Pharaoh come together within us.

As we drove the freeway back to LA, I thought about how Moses and Pharaoh slug it out in every one of us: the one that wants to be free and the one that feels safe in bondage. The folks in jail thought that they would be free when their time was up; the folks out there thought they were free. Just like the children of Israel kept wanting to return to the comforts and certainty of Egypt; addicts have euphoric recall about using and returning to the safety of drugs and the bondage of their lifestyles.

〜

High Holidays with inmates took on a whole new dimension. When the Rabbi discussed *t'shuvah*—the Jewish belief in atonement, transformation and redemption, return—and talked about sin and the gates of life it wasn't an abstraction anymore. Those sins were real. Those gates clanked and shut and open all the time.

Every day.

I learned that the Jewish mystics believed God put t'shuvah into the world before the creation of man as an act of merciful recognition of human imperfection, because he knew that his human creation—part animal and part angel and endowed with free will —would continually sin and would need a path back. I learned that all human beings have good and evil inclinations that battle for dominance. The Talmud resolved this paradox by declaring the good inclination to be good and the evil inclination to be VERY GOOD! I knew from reading Jung that all humans have a shadow. That the brighter the persona, the darker the shadow.

Wow.

Why didn't I know this? Why hadn't anyone taught me this kind of relevant Judaism? Nobody I knew, knew this. As a kid in High Holiday services, we sneered at the fools who went to temple to show off their mink coats and were hypocritical in all their affairs. But most of the temple-goers didn't know this either. They read the prayers on command, endured the boredom of the service, and left unchanged inside. But this proposed that the purpose of spirituality and religion is to develop an inner life you can live with, that frees you to build and maintain your outer life.

In Hebrew, t'shuvah is the word for the action step of dealing with our mistakes and negative impulses. In Jewish mystic thought, t'shuvah was put into the world before God created man. T'shuvah resolves God's dilemma of Free Will: If man were created part human and part divine, free to choose between doing God's will or doing only his own will, he would inevitably make bad choices and need a way to restore himself to balance. The steps of t'shuvah are amazingly similar to the steps of AA. Both require that you admit your wrongdoing, take responsibility for it, make amends to those you have harmed and have a plan to not repeat the misdeed.

Judaism refers to the good inclination and the evil inclination, as *Yetzer Tov* and *Yetzer Hara*: the angel self and the animal self embedded in each of us. To be human is to walk a balance beam between opposing inclinations.

The Rabbis had a paradoxical solution to this duality. They taught that the good inclination is good and the evil inclination is very good. Both come from God and each inclination has a purpose. The challenge of being a human being is to harness the power of the evil or dark side and redirect it to the service of God and good through taking right action.

There's a Midrash I love that lays it out: God has made the animals and the angels and is about to quit creating when He gets an idea. He goes to the angels and says, "Let's make man in our image, and give him Free Will." The angels try to talk Him out of it. "It's a big mistake, God; he'll make bad choices and mess up big time." But God doesn't listen. "I'll give him an instruction manual on how to manage his Free Will and I'll give him t'shuvah, a way to redeem himself when he makes bad choices." Torah is the manual.

One source led to another and I found an article by Dr. Rabbi Abraham Twerski (a psychiatrist and Hassidic Rabbi), *Judaism and the 12 Steps*, in which he koshered AA. Recovering Jews, especially secular ones and even my clients, were sketchy about AA. The meetings were held in church basements and they talked about Christ and said the Lord's Prayer.

Rabbi Twerski outlined the corresponding concepts in Torah that supported the 12 Steps and admitted he found more spirituality at meetings than he found at his Shul. Dr. Twerski combined AA with therapy as the treatment of choice for addicts and alcoholics. This was a revolutionary idea from a Hassidic psychiatrist. I "fell in love" with him.

T'Shuvah, like the 12 Steps, promised redemption, a process requiring self-examination, a searching and fearless moral inventory, admission of wrongdoings, direct amends to whoever has been harmed by one's transgressions and a plan of action not to repeat the behavior. Dr. Twerski prescribed spirituality as the Vitamin C to cure the scurvy of the soul! That metaphor gave me courage and ammunition to challenge the strict medical model of treatment that governed mental health institutions.

Yisrael literally means "he who wrestles with God." I understood this as a moment-to-moment struggle to do the next right thing (even when you don't want to), to act yourself into right thinking and feeling, and to balance the urgings of good and evil inclinations-- Yetzer Tov and Yetzer Hara.

I was electrified by my initiation into the spiritual realm, glimpsing the existence of a Higher Order of Intelligence that gave life meaning and purpose, and made sense of absurdity and adversity. I personally felt relieved of a lot of shame in knowing that everything I had been and done was in some way Godly.

I found a text by Maimonides—*Hilchot T'shuvah*—that I interpreted as the Jewish version of the steps to recovery. The Rabbis said once t'shuvah is made and accepted that person is forgiven and should be seen as blameless. Furthermore, one who has fallen and been redeemed holds a higher place in the Divine realm than one who has never fallen.

This was a view of Judaism I could embrace.

I knew my criminals were going to love this shit.

ADDICTION TO REDEMPTION

Another small, still voice came out of nowhere: *Find a need and fill it.*

I don't think I actually said—*what?* But I heard it again.

Find a need and fill it.

The need wasn't a mystery, but filling it was.

I kept seeing the same people returning to prison. The recidivism rate was 90%. Almost every one of my clients had sworn to me they would never come back to that miserable, de-humanizing place; they'd turn it around. They were released with nothing: no money, no clothes, no car, no phone, no hope. No wonder they were "in the spoon by noon." I called agency after agency, and became as frustrated as they were. There was never a space. I was as helpless to help them, as they were to help themselves.

One chilly morning, Josh, a young guy I'd visited a few times at County, waited outside my office at the hospital. He was shivering in shorts and tank-top. He'd been busted in the summer and it's all he had. Josh's father was a psychiatrist. I asked him if he'd called his family, but after years of his craziness and failures, they wouldn't even take his calls anymore.

He needed a rehab. I gave him coffee and a bagel, and then I opened the resource directory and started at the top.

"May I speak to your intake worker, please? My name is Harriet Rossetto, and I'm a social worker with the Jewish Committee for Personal Service. I have a young man sitting right here who needs to get into a program ASAP... Uh-huh. What's he supposed to do for three weeks? How can he call you every morning when he has no place to stay and no money for a phone call? I'm sorry, I know it's not your fault; can you recommend someplace that might have a bed?... Thanks, anyway."

I called every program in Los Angeles, the San Fernando Valley and Glendale-Pasadena, and the responses were all some version of the same: Call tomorrow. Get on the waiting list. Show up at 6 a.m. Does he have insurance?

Finally I scored. The Royal Palms would have an opening in the morning. I only had to find a bed for the night. I remembered reading that Jewish Family Service had received FEMA money for transitional living and could provide vouchers for homeless people. We take care of our own, don't we?

"Hi, may I speak with your intake worker? Hi, Sylvia, this is Harriet, a social worker at Gateways Hospital... I need a hotel voucher for a young man who just got out of jail. Yes, he's Jewish, his father's a doctor... What do you mean long-term treatment plan? My long-term treatment plan is a bed for tonight."

I told her to go fuck herself.

Josh sat there calmly. He wasn't angry or surprised. I sensed that he was actually relieved, freed from his attempt to change his life by our inability to help him. He knew it, he just came to reassure himself he really had no options.

There were hundreds of Joshes and Janes released with no place to go except backwards to the life they knew. I knew I couldn't spend my days calling programs with three-week waiting lists that tested an addict's willingness by demanding that he call every morning by 7 a.m. to assure his place on the list.

～

In the 1980's, FEMA (the Federal Emergency Management Act) was dumping big pots of money into Los Angeles to hide the homeless. I had been ignoring the official "RFP's" (requests for proposal) to access some of that money to open a shelter. My clients weren't exactly homeless: they were in jail. And the government application forms were designed to discourage all but the severely obsessive-compulsive.

But how to fill the need came clear when I found a piece of paper buried in the piles on my desk. They were giving money away for a one-time purchase of a building to be used as a homeless shelter. Since most of my guys became homeless upon release, it could work as a release program. The paper promised that the regulatory agencies would ease the process and permits as a way to encourage agencies to apply. So under the aegis of my employer—Gateways Hospital— I applied.

I crafted a proposal about a post-prison residential stay where the Jewish felons I'd been visiting in jail, could—upon release— pull themselves together. A Jewish home, based on love and learning, where wounded people could heal their broken souls and reconnect with their families, themselves and God. It would be a place of 12 Steps, Judaism and psychotherapy, a place to re-integrate into a meaningful life. They could make t'shuvah: admit their wrongdoing, make amends and restitution, and plan how not to re-offend, to make different choices.

I would call it Beit T'Shuvah—House of Return/Repentance.

~

I filled out the paperwork optimistically, but was off guard when the award letter actually arrived. It gave us less than a month to close escrow on a property. I didn't even know what an escrow actually was. Suddenly I was taking meetings with realtors and title companies and attorneys, and studying tract maps and talking zoning laws and county audits. I had a good ear and I was a good mimic and understood *fake it till you make it.*

Before long, we owned a three-story house at 216 South Lake Street in one of the worst neighborhoods in Los Angeles. No one mentioned that I had taken possession of a fully occupied property with no clue that the law required us to pay $3,000 each to relocate—per person, not per unit. In the midst of my panic I had to laugh. I just got a grant from the Feds to open a homeless shelter, and in order to do so, I had to drive these people from their homes. Right before Christmas, too.

We worked it out by giving free rent for two months.

The place looked uninhabitable, like one of those photos when some slumlord gets busted. But when I looked hard I detected evidence of youthful beauty in leaded glass windows, original mahogany, and ornate moldings. And on the ground floor to the right of the front door was a two-room unit where the manager lived. It had a large bay window that looked out on the porch and let in light, and a mantel where the fireplace had been, French doors to the hallway. It made me happy. I claimed it as my office/ sitting room.

I had no staff, a vague program and no budget for operating expenses. I promised the Gateways Board that all it would cost them would be food, utilities and my salary: under $50,000 per year. I couldn't leave the residents alone in the house at night— they'd turn it into a shooting gallery. I'd have to move in for awhile until the first harvest yielded a survivor I could trust to be a resident manager.

I walked out to the porch to smoke and survey the situation, when I noticed Stanley, a jail client, walking up the path. It was pre-cell phones. He got an early kick-out and called my office. They told him where I was and what was going on, and he found me.

"Look at this mess," he said, kicking a piece of rotting wood. "I used to be a contractor, you know…"

I was his salvation and he was mine. That happened a lot.

Expect a miracle.

I brought Stanley coffee and a bagel every morning, never sure I'd find him there, or what or who else I might find. Gang graffiti appeared on fresh paint and drug dealers stood sentry on every corner, responding to some invisible signal that directed them when to sell, when to swallow and when to stash and run.

In the spirit of neighbor relations I approached the one I sensed was the shot-caller, and introduced myself. I was becoming an everyday event and after a few weeks we couldn't pretend not to notice one another. We progressed from imperceptible nods to eye contact and good mornings.

"Excuse me. My name is Harriet. I don't want to make trouble, but this is a rehab. I'd appreciate it if you didn't sell to the folks here."

"Lady, I respect what you're doing. I'm only doing this so I can send money to my family in El Savador. We'll watch your back and your car and tell you if they try to score."

I knew better than to throw my arms around him, but I did give him a God bless you and meant it.

I made a far out I-and-thou connection with a gangbanging Salvadorean drug dealer in broad daylight in the middle of Lake Street in the Rampart district of Los Angeles. Me. I had always been timid, afraid to be alone, triple dead-bolting myself in my apartment, sleeping with lights on. And now I had the chutzpa to move into a house with thieves and junkies in the worst neighborhood in Los Angeles?

Yup, I had that chutzpa.

And I was fucking loving it.

Marty, Henry and Paul arrived with their various stories and issues, in the same week and moved in to help Stanley finish painting.

Stanley was agitated, pacing the porch as I arrived with his coffee. "We got trouble… these guys got drunk and partied all night with some Strawberry they brought home."

"What's a strawberry?"

"A crack whore."

"Where are they now?"

"They've passed out in there. The hooker left."

"Well, let's go wake them up and throw them out."

They were, of course, morning-after contrite and scared—the disease made them do it, they got it out of their system, never do it again, one more chance… blah blah blah.

I let it go. I accepted the responsibility for expecting newly freed convicts and addicts to be capable of self-regulation and leaving them unsupervised. I let them stay, but moved in that day. I took over the house manager's "suite," sleeping on a couch in my office.

I mapped out the activities and the rules for living together, the Derech Eretz. We would begin each day with a morning meditation and inspirational readings from the AA. *Day At A Time* book and The *12 Steps of Jewish Recovery*. Then we would work on fixing up the house and chores and one of them each week would come with me to the supermarket. Friday night we would light candles and I would prepare Shabbat dinner and we would sit around the table and discuss the meaning of life.

There was a sad irony behind my inspired planning. I hadn't ever created that kind of orderly "Jewish home" or spiritual life or grounded meaningfulness for myself and my daughter, in our own home. In fact, it was chaotic and messy, lacking spirit. But somehow with coke dealers, molesters, frauds, and gangsters it was a divine mission.

The Sunday morning following our first Shabbaton I woke up on the couch in my office and reached for my glasses and jewelry.

The glasses were there. My gold bracelet, a confirmation gift, and my grandmother's engagement ring were gone.

I crawled around the room, looking under everything, closing my eyes and telling myself that when I opened them and looked back at the night table they would magically reappear. The awful truth wormed its way up through layers of magical thinking and denial.

You knew I was a snake when you took me in.

But bite the hand that feeds you?

They stole from their families; why wouldn't they steal from me? I pounded up the stairs and kicked open the door of the first bedroom."Everybody up against the wall, right now." Henry and Paul sat up; Jimmy feigned sleep. "You too, asshole."

"What's up; what'sa matter, Mom?"

"Don't Mom me. Where is it?"

"Where's what?"

"Look, we'll pretend this is kindergarten. I'll close my eyes and you all tiptoe downstairs and put my jewelry back where you found it."

"Somebody took your jewelry? Who coulda done a thing like that? Come on, guys, we'll help her find it."

I laughed, remembering the description of a junky I had just heard: "A junky is someone who steals your money and then helps you look for it."

I felt like a moronic Alice-in-Wonderland who believed that chicken soup could really restore the soul. I realized I was in over my head and needed help.

Harlan "The Monk" Levey appeared in the nick of time—a short, fat, bald, bow-legged man—huffing and puffing up the street. Just released from Federal prison after 29 years. I made him house manager on the spot—room, board and $150 per week. Harlan was savvy and streetwise, an 800-pound gorilla with a heart of gold. He cooked and cleaned, shopped and convinced the boys he knew what they were up to before they were up to it, happy to be the enforcer.

My jewelry never reappeared.

∼

I moved back to my apartment and spent most of my days in jail, prison or court, spreading the word that we now had a place for Jews coming out of jails and prisons or needing an alternative to incarceration. Within a few months, all 25 beds were full and the calls kept coming from defense attorneys, prison chaplains and inmates about to be released.

Every day there was a new true crime novella or documentary to challenge or titillate me. I was having such a good time I felt like I should be paying Gateways for the opportunity. I was never bored, never lonely or insignificant.

Suddenly, like alchemy, the qualities that had made me feel like a misfit all my life, now made me a hero.

∼

Emboldened by success, I placed an ad in the *Los Angeles Times*: "Looking for a needle-in-a-haystack. Rabbi/social worker needed for half-way house." A letter arrived two days later: "Dear Madam, I am your needle." He was perfect: ordained, MSW, Kabbalistic Tevye-like, to the Greek fisherman's cap! I hired him on the spot. Soon after, small items started disappearing from residents' rooms. They accused each other until the rabbi was discovered in the women's dorm, taking toothpaste and underwear. God sends a kleptomaniac rabbi to a half-way house for Jewish criminals? That was my lesson in the difference between magical and mystical. I needed to learn that things are not always what they seem to be and that the healers can be wounded. And that God has a hell of a sense of humor!

I also needed to check references.

Then Rabbi Mel Silverman's group at Chino State Prison heard about us. His "congregation" had a lot of questions and invited me to the prison for a presentation, if you can call it that.

There were about fifteen riled up inmates. The Rabbi's clerk, Mark Borovitz—who I'd seen around before—was particularly interested and appointed himself spokesperson for the group. Did I know what they needed? The obstacles they faced? We were all sitting in a circle and he starts yelling. Loud. Gruff. Rude. I don't remember the particulars, just a lot of questions, challenges. Are you doing this? What about that?

So much for my fantasy of their gratitude. It pissed me off.

After one of the big guy's outbursts, I said, "Listen, I'm out there trying to make this work. If you know so much, smartass, when you get out of here, why don't you come help me?"

It wasn't like this-is-your-soulmate was blinking in glowing neon on his chest.

It wasn't a small, still voice saying—this is going to be your partner, your husband, your co-visionary, a Rabbi-in-the-making.

Nope. That day I just thought he was an arrogant asshole.

~

Now that I had beds for my addicts, I—advertently—became the queen of "alternative sentencing."

Defense attorneys were so desperate for viable alternatives to incarceration that I got cases that stretched the definition of addiction further and further. And I made them.

I presented a computer hacker to a Federal Judge as an addict and won the case, earning my 15 minutes of fame for being the first ever to do that. Even Connie Chung called. He was trapped in the addictive cycle as much any druggie or compulsive gambler, powerless over hacking. He didn't do it for money. It was his way out of himself, providing comfort, excitement, and a sense of purpose that eluded him in ordinary life, filling the "hole in his soul": Addiction.

I stood before a judge for George, a 50-year old engineer and accountant who'd embezzled over $100,000 from the company where he was comptroller. I had written a comprehensive sentencing report explaining George's theft as a by-product of his compulsive gambling, recommending treatment and restitution as an alternative to incarceration.

I'd been visiting George in County Jail since his arrest two months previously but this was my first meeting with his parents,

Solomon and Sylvia. I saw the ambush in their eyes—How could this happen? Phi Beta Kappa from Cornell. A "good son" who visited every week. The father was a Holocaust survivor, almost 90, had been Man of Honor at his synagogue and received a proclamation from the Governor.

He, like many parents of my clients, wondered how a man with a Governor's proclamation could have a son handcuffed to five other men who they would never allow in their home. They didn't know, like I did, that there were hundreds of parents and family members just like them, whose loved ones—suffering from addictions—had fallen off a cliff from a perfect life and golden-child status into a scummy black hole.

Sylvia squeezed my hand: "It'll kill his father if he doesn't come out."

Bruce Kaufman for the defense went first. "Your Honor, I'd like to point out the defendant's family, his wife and parents. His two sons are not present in Court per the family's request. I also have Ms. Rossetto, who prepared the pre-sentence report and has accepted him for long-term residential treatment at the Beit T'Shuvah program."

I nodded to the Judge, who complimented me on my report. "You did your homework, Ms. Rossetto. I understand that the gambler is motivated more by the 'action' than the money, they always walk away broke, it seems; I have a harder time believing that this Cornell Phi Beta Kappa comptroller was 'borrowing' and not stealing the money."

"I understand the problem, Your Honor, but it's not a semantic trick. For the compulsive gambler, the adrenaline rush of being in action distorts perception and impairs judgment just like alcohol or drugs. When they are in action their fears and insecurities are magically transformed into feelings of omnipotence, omniscience and optimism. Their fear of the unknown becomes an illusion of certainty. They are no longer gambling; they know they are going to win and will be able to replace the money before the loss is discovered."

"It's a stretch, Ms. Rossetto."

"Your Honor, what isn't a stretch is that the criminal behavior is inextricably linked to the compulsive gambling, an unintended consequence, if you will. When he is not gambling, George is a responsible, pro-social family man. It is, therefore, in his, his family's and society's best interests to treat the disease. Although I cannot guarantee that he will remain abstinent, I can most assuredly guarantee that if he is not treated he will re-offend, but if he is treated he will make full restitution. I'll monitor him closely, Your Honor. If he fails to comply, prison is always an option."

The "People," of course, protested: *White-collar crime, is still crime; he can go for treatment when he gets out of prison; large sum of money—over $100,000...*

The Judge sighed in resignation. "Ok, Ms. Rossetto, you got him for a year. Don't embarrass me, George. If I ever see you in this Court again, I'll throw the book at you."

We walked outside the Courtroom. Solomon kissed my hand with tears rolling down his cheeks. Sylvia took my face in both her hands and kissed me on both cheeks. The defense attorney patted me on the back, "I couldn't have done this without you."

Talk about an adrenaline rush. I was hooked forever. Viktor Frankl spoke to me from the grave. My search for meaning was over.

I had found it.

YOU MATTER

*I*t's winter, 1988.

The small, still voices forgot to mention the overwhelming day-to-day bullshit—the hardcore realities of having 25 transitioning, recovering felons under one leaky roof, of lack of funds and services, tiny staff.

We're still in Beit T'Shuvah's first location—the screens are torn, the porch is rotted, it's filthy—but I'm incredibly proud of it. I stay open for business. Somehow help comes, in all kinds of forms.

There's a knock on the door.

It's Mark—the 300 lb. loud-mouth from Chino who pissed me off, Rabbi Silverman's assistant. He's standing there in a torn Jolly Green Giant sweatsuit that barely covers his white belly. I just stare. He stares back, glances around my office.

"You said I should come see you when I get out. I'm out. Remember?"

He thinks I don't recognize him, but I do. What I am, is surprised. I'm a social worker whose clients are criminals and addicts. Follow-up isn't their strong suit.

He wants a job.

I know I have to be careful. He's a serial con; I'm a serial trust-er. His only asset is the $200 gate money from Chino. He has no car, no clothes but what he's wearing. But I remember that Pauline gave him her blessing after we left Chino one day. She said, "That Mark Borovitz, he's no schlepper."

I decide to risk it. I take Pauline's "he's-no-schlepper" comment as a reference. Anyway, I need the help.

"You can fix up and manage the thrift shop. The offer is part-time, minimum wage, all I can afford for now. You'll organize items, do pricing, that kind of thing."

He's thrilled.

I'm wary.

About a week later we have our grand opening. I arrive with all twenty Beit T'Shuvah residents, and smile when I walk in the door. It's great—tables for everything, stuff nicely arranged and with price tags. Like a real store. I'm impressed.

Watchful, but impressed.

~

For the next few months we'd drink coffee and read the newspapers in my office each morning before work. He was excited about what Beit T'Shuvah could be and we talked a lot about the future.

We did outreach presentations at synagogues where Mark told his story, and I talked the mission. Mark rocked Friday night services, just like he does now, and they became a hit, as did the Wednesday Morning Torah study group. When my secretary fell off the wagon, I gave him the gig—a little more money and full time!

I noticed symmetries that seemed almost spooky. We both lost our only and best-friend fathers when we were 14, and it altered the course of our lives and well-being: irrevocably. They were the ones who 'got' us, made us 'feel felt.' We were both fat, klutzy kids who were left out. We shared the same underdog view of the world, laughed at the same jokes and had the same heroes. Our core wounds, core strengths, and core interests (politics, books, films, music, and Judaic thought…) were extremely—and oddly—compatible, especially for two people with so many surface differences like age and experiences and which side of the prison glass we'd sat behind.

But I didn't let myself forget that Mark was a felon, and like all the guys at Beit T'Shuvah: just out of jail, returning to life on the outside. It's a sketchy, tough transition. Not everyone makes it. I was his boss. We had an intense friendship. I kept it that way. But there was something, a spark—it didn't have a name, it wasn't romantic, but it was soulful. It existed and took shape as inspired involvement with Beit T'Shuvah, as being searchers, passionate learners and excited by new ideas.

As in all love stories, there are many reasons, decisions, and nuances on the journey from there to here. Your life is rocked, and everything changes, but you don't always know it's happening—just like with miracles. You do, but you don't.

What I do know, is that I felt felt.

Mark made some hard decisions after trying to reconnect to his former life and his family and marriage. He asked for a divorce. A painful, complicated thing because he loved his daughter more than anything, and felt responsible to his wife and guilt over what he'd put them through. But his soul was on fire, going somewhere he hadn't ever been.

He sensed that his future required a focused spiritual life so he could make penance, so he could teach his story about how a nice Jewish boy who grew up almost orthodox and went to services every Friday night, fell so far from grace. And also, he needed to study Judaism in a serious way.

That, too, was strangely compatible to what I was building at Beit T'Shuvah. Unconsciously, and before anything romantic, we formed the foundations of the partnership and leadership we have today: I was out getting money and services, putting together a staff, and he was the go-getter, getting Beit T'Shuvah on the map. We were both defining, envisioning and going— toward an unknown future.

Eventually, I learned about another decision Mark had made about his life.

After work one night, I came home from a bad blind date, and Mark was waiting on the porch, holding a red rose. It sparked.

That was the moment the relationship shifted to romantic. I am an inside outlaw: "nice Jewish girl" on the outside, "not-so-nice" inside; the perfect mate for a not-so-nice Jewish outlaw with a prophetic soul. And yeah, I broke all my own rules and all the rules of good sense—again. We went from soulmates to roommates, very fast. It was a crazy time. But now that we've been married over 20 years, I can say it worked out.

In those early days of Beit T'Shuvah, we were searchers and seekers and had a keen sense we were building something bigger than ourselves.

~

My journey to faith continued—however imperfect, eclectic and haphazard—evolving from concepts and thoughts, to practical applications and clinical ways to repair souls: my own and my clients'.

I continued to read everything, took classes, experimented with paradoxical interventions, practiced on myself. I asked a lot of questions of people who seemed wise. I learned that although religious practices differ and can separate people, spiritual wisdom is universal and connects people to themselves and one another.

My mind was being stretched almost every day to embrace the dissociated extremes of human beings and reflect back to them the possibility of one-ness, wholeness. Mark was experiencing the same extremes, battling for their souls. He used the Torah texts to ferret out their secrets, scrape the barnacles off their souls. As he showed them who they had been and who they could become he showed himself too, and we grew in intimacy and authenticity by sharing our self-revelations with one another. We both loved the existential suspense, the "24-7" action, the daily dramas, the wild ride.

One of the most important lessons I had learned was that whatever someone does to someone else they will eventually do to you, and when Mark and I first got together, I paid close attention. Most of the times I'd been conned or ripped off it was my own hubris in believing "he would never do it to me."

But I was beginning to trust Mark's loyalty to those who had helped him, and he was also a poster boy for our mission: transformation is possible. He was a convert to decency and integrity, and he wasn't for sale, even though I could see he was a glutton for attention. He was also like a girlfriend, patiently shopping for clothes with a good eye for what was "me" and what wasn't, and talking for hours about feelings and people-watching (with commentary) in the best yenta tradition. He cooked and cleaned and made sure to get up before me to make coffee and bring me breakfast in bed—but wait, wait, hold it, be careful! Remember Carl Jung—"The brighter the persona the darker the shadow." Shards of Mark's shadow began to puncture the surface, as did mine.

One of the smartest things we did (without really knowing what we were doing) is that we put a spiritual foundation in place for our relationship and our work life. And it started with our discovery of Jonathan Omer-Man, a Rabbi teaching classes and workshops in Los Angeles.

Our bonding took shape in a spiritual framework, and although there's no word for it, we viewed ourselves in a kind of holy mission and we knew it would sustain our connection. God is still our marriage counselor!

~

Rabbi Jonathan Omer-Man came to Los Angeles to re-ignite Jewish kids seduced by cults and to teach classes in spirituality. The first night Mark and I read Mishna: "Make for yourself a teacher, choose for yourself a friend and give each man the benefit of the doubt." Without discussing it, each of us made Jonathan our teacher, giving him the power to guide each of us separately and prepare us to come together as whole and holy souls.

He also wisely decided to re-program Judaism to stem the flow of Jews seeking spirituality outside of Judaism, particularly in Buddhism, called JUBU's. His friend, Rodger Kamenetz, wrote a book called *The Jew in the Lotus*, and another called *Stalking Elijah* (which had a chapter on Mark referring to him as a mystical master—even before he became a Rabbi!).

Because of his humility and integrity we didn't fight over Jonathan, compete for his attention or deify him. He self-disclosed, exposed his weaknesses and vulnerabilities and refused to take himself (or anyone else) too seriously. As I watched him arrange his legs after he settled into his chair or pull himself up onto his crutches, I felt ashamed of my whining. When he admonished me about going "so quickly to despair," I realized I could choose not to do that.

The realization that I could overpower the despair that still "crouched at my door" and stole my joy liberated me from a lifetime of gloom and doom. The negative thoughts that Jonathan called "voluntary suffering" as opposed to "necessary pain." There were many firsts and lessons we attribute to those days with "our" teacher and mentor and friend. I can't say why, but we felt anointed by Jonathan to help carry this message of Jewish spiritual healing to the afflicted and addicted Los Angeles Jewish Community.

Jonathan and a small group of Jews met with the Dalai Lama and the JUBU denomination was added to the list. He taught classes in meditation and mysticism and was available for spiritual counseling. Mark and I both "fell in love" with Jonathan and through him, fell in love with each other. Jonathan embodied intellect and wisdom, devotion and irreverence. Although crippled by polio and dependent on crutches, he walked his talk and helped us do the same. Some of his precepts have become part of ours and were life-altering insights: *Most people go to psychiatrists for what are essentially spiritual problems; suffering is voluntary, pain is essential; happiness is an obligation.*

Jonathan knew our souls and knew what teachings and spiritual practices each of us needed. Mark vibrated to the warriors and Prophets. I resonated to the peacemakers and Psalmists. We were enthusiastic students, on fire with learning and missionary zeal. We passed on Jonathan's teaching to the students at Beit T'Shuvah and witnessed transformation in them as well.

The Mishnah of Ben Zoma said it all: *Who is Rich? He who rejoices in his portion. Who is Wise? He who learns from everyone. Who is Mighty? He who masters his passions. Who is deserving of Honor? He who honors everyone.*

That was a huge one. My clients didn't just dishonor others, they dishonored themselves. Many not only lost control, but they didn't care anymore. Over and over I'd hear: "What difference does it make?" "Why bother?" "Fuck It." "It's their fault, not mine." These are the mottos of addiction.

Lacking self care and avoiding oneself and one's responsibilities takes enormous energy; it saps the spirit and causes us to seek distraction, comfort or consolations in bad things. Drugs, alcohol, food, gambling, sex, shopping or even self-mutilations soothe us. You are absolved of responsibility. The will to change or act becomes anaesthetized, commanding more and more substances, stimuli and stuff to keep it from awakening.

Why bother to make your bed every day when it's going to get messed up very night? Why bother to exercise or eat right or have a mammogram when you know you're going to get old and die? Why fold the laundry and put it away only to have to repeat the cycle every week? Or get the car washed or clean the house or all the other up-keeps of daily life?

In Christian theology, the word is *Acedia*—one of the 7 Deadly Sins, connoting not just a lack of care, but profound indifference.

The Benedictine Monks called it the Noon-Day Demon, the voice that whispers: Why bother? The refusal to engage with life is an affliction of the soul that leads to paralysis of effort. It is the despair borne of the belief that nothing matters. It is a denial of the gift of life.

Psychology often labels this indifference as depression. We medicate it or look for cognitive solutions. These interventions target the brain and mind and there is no doubt that they are important. However, I began to see acedia as a dis-ease of the soul requiring the daily discipline of spiritual practice as well.

I can't quote sources, chapter or verse, but my Judaism—shaped by all these new thoughts—started to rest on a few core beliefs that helped me redefine my perception of myself, of others and of the purpose of life.

I matter.
You matter.
I have a holy soul.
I am imperfect by design.
My value is a birthright.
Change is possible and mandatory.
Right action is the bridge to wholeness of self.

My former negative view of life—nothing matters, who cares—had been shifting anyway, now it went 180: everything mattered, I realized. Everything.

As Rabbi Abraham Joshua Heschel wrote: *something sacred is at stake in every event.*

ROGUE RABBI & REBEL REBBETZIN

In January of 1996, I read an article in the *Jewish Journal* about the University of Judaism receiving a secret donation to open a Rabbinic School on the West Coast.

The small, still voice was whispering again.

This time I was "paying attention" with full knowledge of what it means to "expect a miracle." And I knew it was going to be a miracle, and I knew it was going to be huge. But I didn't realize just how miraculous, and just how big and like a lot of things this particular miracle engendered: just how tough.

I stared at Mark.

He stared back.

"What?"

I handed the paper over.

The thought of becoming a Rabbi's wife was still in the fun, uncomplicated fantasy stage. I wasn't yet forced to think about my passion for unkosher fried calamari, or my favorite Sabbath junket of mani-pedi followed by shopping at Costco.

"You're already a Rabbi—it means teacher, right? It's what you do best, what you love most, go for it. They're designing it for change of career people, like you, searching for meaning… I'll bet you're the only one who's changing from criminal to Rabbi— it's usually the other way around."

He tossed it on the table, and walked out.

I'm thinking win-win: free cruises, parsonage tax deductions on the house. Mark would have a cool diploma on the wall to give legitimacy to what he was doing anyway—teaching, spiritual counseling, leading services—give us legitimacy for the Beit T'Shuvah board and community at large. I wasn't thinking of the fears and doubts Mark was experiencing in the face of having to "sell" himself to traditional, conservative rabbis and academics who would judge him and his bad choices, his t'shuvah, his potential, and whether he was worth the risk. Or not.

I shouted so he could hear: "Find out the application deadline!"

By the next afternoon both his Rabbis, Jonathan and Ed, echoed the same thing, independently, and he decided to go for it— with less than two weeks to take the G.R.E., gather transcripts and references and write his "Why I want to be a Rabbi" autobiography. He delivered the final application package one hour before the 5 p.m. cut off. He said he didn't care whether they accepted or rejected him, but I noticed his edge—he yelled more, prayed more and spent more time playing spider solitaire on his computer. Team Borovitz kicked in. Rabbi Ed Feinstein helped prepare him mentally; I took him shopping for a suit, shoes, shirt and tie and bought him a new kippa; the residents of Beit T'Shuvah and our friends prayed for him and promised to picket the school if he wasn't accepted.

He thought he "aced" the interview and forced them to confront themselves in considering his candidacy: did they believe in t'shuvah or not and if they did, did they believe his t'shuvah was complete?

I tried to imagine the committee's post-interview debate about unorthodox candidate, Borovitz. "We need a guy like him to reach our kids … Jewish continuity, redemption. But… but how do we know he won't relapse, embarrass us, diminish our credibility? Will we be able to control him? What about our donors?

As we waited for the decision, there was still Beit T'Shuvah and the 24/7/365 crises—dramas of relapses, arrests, jail releases, Federation missions and speaking engagements.

One night we opened Shabbat to the Federation honchos as we embarked on a major campaign to expand. The "tent" in the backyard where we held services rain or shine was becoming our trademark; a symbol of pioneering spirit and grass roots spirituality, an urban kibbutz in the barrio, a tent in the desert where the sounds of *Shma Yisrael* mixed with sirens, gunfire and hovering helicopters every Friday night. Searchlights flashed over the tent, illuminating the faces of nice Jewish boys and girls standing to give gratitude for being Jewish and being at Beit T'Shuvah. All the families and volunteers who came were touched in a place they didn't even know they had. It was a stormy night and the small group of wealthy philanthropists got their feet soaked as the tent flapped and water puddled. The patio heaters warmed the first few rows but most of the congregation shivered. In spite of all that, the amazing seeds of our first major Capital Campaign were planted that night and took hold.

On a Friday afternoon in March, at about 3 p.m., Mark called. "I stopped home to get the mail. It's here!"

"What does it say?"

"I don't know; I'm afraid to open it."

"Is it fat or thin? … OPEN IT, for Christ sake!" We held our breath as he opened the envelope. I waited, I waited…

"I'm here, Mark," I told him. I wanted him to know—here, no matter what, yes or no, bad or good. I was here for him. Always.

"Ready?"

"Ready."

"Dear Mark, we are pleased to inform you… I'm in!"

I shouted to everybody in the building: "He's in! He's in! Mark got accepted to Rabbinic school."

The whoops and shouts collided throughout the house. It was a communal triumph: all of us had been accepted.

The mood in the tent that night was higher than any drug. We were one, not by might and not by power, but by spirit alone, our Rabbi, Mark Borovitz—ex-con, human being, and spiritual leader of a band of raggle-taggle misfits and rejects would be ordained in four years, May, 2000 as a REAL RABBI.

As he spoke his gratitude that night at services he looked right at me… "I am most grateful to share this victory with my wife, without whom this miracle could never have happened, and to see in her eyes that her faith in me has been rewarded. You, my dear, are a true Eshet Chayil, woman of valor.

That night I was really happy to be his woman of valor and Rebbetzin-to-be.

But that was before reality hit.

~

We're at the University of Judaism, the first meet-up with his new classmates and spouses for a traditional Shabboton weekend in the dorms. University of Judaism is not new-agey, JUBU-ish Rabbi School. It's full-on traditional, conservative training: year in Israel, texts in Hebrew. Ok. Not quite big hats and full beards, but it's way closer to Modern Orthodox than to the reform movement.

I look around. Like Jewish camp, but grown ups. I immediately feel my old, childhood misfit status. They know the songs, prayers and when to say them; when to stand and when to sit. I don't.

We file into the Dining Room for the Friday night Kosher meal. I make it through candle lighting, Kiddish and motzi—as if I belong. Then everyone stands up to wash their hands at a basin in the corner of the room. They pour water from a pitcher, say a prayer and return silently to their seats, not speaking, waiting until everyone is finished. I interpret smiles as holy smirks.

Mark stands up and joins the line. Traitor! He's one of them now? Washing hands is not our custom. I hadn't learned that prayer. Should I go through the motions and mumble something? Or just sit and draw attention to myself as a heretic? Will my actions or non-actions give Mark a black mark?

The what-am-I-in-for realization that this Rabbi thing is a thing, and is going to seriously impact my life is creeping into my consciousness. This is not just about the Hanukkah All Aboard Cancun tour.

I excuse myself and go outside for a cigarette.

I don't know if I can do this. I make a mental list of things to tell Mark that I refuse to do as a Rabbi's wife. I'm not going to freak out if I mix up milk and meat dishes, or run around my house with a feather, hunting hametz before Pesach. And the things I will do: I will continue to get my nails done Saturday morning. And then I will go to Costco, by car, and spend money. It's my ritual I look forward to all week and I'm not changing it—that's Shabbos to me. I'll move out before I agree to give up fried calamari!

The next day we learn real Jews don't eat breakfast Shabbos morning either—or make coffee! Lunch after services is the first meal and two more meals follow, the third one with some name I can't pronounce, which means the third meal. No coffee?

"Let's go out," I say.

Mark's caught in a conundrum. The tables are turned. Most of the time he's our boundary tester. This time, I'm leading us toward temptation.

"C'mon Mark. One latte..."

"We'll get caught if we drive and there's nothing within walking distance," he says.

But I've had it. I can't find any spiritual significance in being deprived of my morning coffee.

Even I get that it's about the coffee and it's not about the coffee. It's about who I am, who will I be. More importantly: who will we be?

I love the idea of Shabbos as a scheduled time of inner direction and reflection. I agree with Thomas Cahill that it's the gift from the Jews to the world. But it infuriates me that everyone seems to focus more on the rules and rituals rather than on the spiritual significance, actually killing their own spirits as they judge the validity of each other's practices. "My observance is better than yours."

We had a young Orthodox crack addict at Beit T'Shuvah whose mother became hysterical when he refused to wear a kippa when he came home, because if the neighbors saw him that would disqualify her daughter from making a good marriage.

Seriously....????

I react defensively when people ask: "Is Beit T'Shuvah kosher?" "I'm Koshering their souls, not their stomachs," I say. "Besides, Kosher meat costs three times what we pay and no one has offered to donate it."

I make an illicit call to our friends who live nearby. They invite us for coffee and breakfast. We grab another couple and sneak out like naughty children, crouching behind parked cars, covering our mouths to prevent giggles. We're back in time for morning prayers.

Later that afternoon, there's a meeting for spouses to bond and share concerns about the next four years, and the challenges and pressures of being married to a Rabbi. The conversation quickly turns to levels of observance and keeping kosher. Several of the women have young children and one mother boasts that she no longer allows her children to play with Reformed Jewish children because her kids might inadvertently be introduced to cheeseburgers.

I'm thinking—cheeseburgers, you asshole! We're saving souls, counseling parents whose kids are dead, homeless, or sitting in County jail, and you're worried about cheeseburgers?

Then one by one, we say what we will do differently after the weekend. And it's my turn.

"What I'm going to do differently...?" I look around the room.

"I'm going to file for divorce."

I had to chuckle at God's sense of humor. I finally find a Jewish bad boy and he's going to become a RABBI!

~

With Jonathan's help we eventually worked out the details of our "mixed marriage."

I could do Costco by myself on Saturday or with him on Sunday. In therapy I had insisted that I wanted to be a "Costco couple," like the other couples I saw, pushing their carts together, helping one another lift the heavy items out of the cart at check-out. Isn't that why you get married? No way I was going to become a *shtetl* housewife doing all the work so my husband could pore over the Holy books all day and not worry about making a living.

And Rabbi issues became relationship issues.

"So how come you smoke on Shabbos and play on your computer?" I shouted. "Isn't that an *averos* (sin) too? Isn't Shabbos just a good reason not to do the things you don't want to do?"

But I wondered if I was obsessing about Costco to force him to choose between me and Shabbos. Did I really enjoy doing Costco together or was it an abstraction, a vestigial fairy-tale about the way it's supposed to be. But I was stubborn: If I could give up Costco on Saturday, he could come on Sundays.

The togetherness reality at Costco meant me getting pissed and frustrated as he got lost in the aisles, distracted by gadgets and electronics and clothes, while I powered my cart through the food and paper goods, trying to get to checkout as quickly as possible. I liked going solo. After two weeks, I switched back to Saturday.

Costco, like the coffee, was a metaphor.

Could I practice my brand of Judaism or was I going to have to convert? My emotions fluctuated between anger at them and fear of losing Mark. Would they brainwash him, rob him of his passion and originality, turn him into a Rabbi 101 functionary? Would he decide he needed a wife who kept Kosher, covered her head and walked to shul in tennis shoes? Would I have to pretend to be *shomer Shabbos* to protect his reputation?

New fights and issues erupted when Mark made the decision to be Kosher. He made no demand that I join him, only that I respect his decision and not have any *tref* meat in the house. He sent up a few balloons about two sets of dishes, which I met with tirades about fanaticism and fundamentalism and hypocrisy. He tried to convey the spiritual significance of making separation and prohibition underlying the practice of *Kashrut*, comparing it to my "Kashrut" of Weight Watchers. I conceded in the abstract but wasn't interested. No more Sunday morning breakfasts at the Pantry? No more KooKooRoo, our favorite restaurant? I'm not going to those greasy, Kosher holes-in-the-wall with linoleum tablecloths and screaming kids with *pais* and *tzitzes*. Forget it.

Eventually I agreed to Kosher-style at home, kosher meats, and mostly vegetarian and soy imitations. He would eat fish in regular restaurants, and I could eat what I wanted, whenever I wanted—outside the house.

I watched Mark struggle with his level of observance, trying to please University of Judaism and to appease me. He embraced the "not yet" philosophy of Franz Rosenzweig—a secular German Jew of the 19th century—who "tried on" observance tentatively. When asked if he observed such and such answered, "Not yet."

A few months into the semester, Mark bought *tzitzes*, the fringed garment mentioned in Torah: "It's a symbolic reminder of God's will, not mine. It protects me against negativity—I'll wear it inside so it doesn't show and you won't be embarrassed." He playfully threatened that he would get a *streimel* (big fur hat) to wear on Shabbos with a long black coat.

For the first time I was comforted by Mark's difficulty sustaining his resolutions and commitments. This, too, would pass. He stopped and started smoking, started and stopped exercising, dieting, hanging up his clothes, or keeping his car clean. The Kosher lasted; the tzitzes didn't. I continued to get my nails done, go to Costco on Saturday and eat calamari fritti in restaurants.

Eventually I came to where I am now: the mindful way that I eat is my *kashrut*. There are things I eat and things I don't eat, mix and don't mix. My kashrut is customized for me, designed to maintain health and self-esteem, to honor my body and nourish my soul.

But as much as we fought about the details—and as much I viewed it as an inconvenient, rigid lifestyle I was programmed to rebel against—I knew this was his essence, mission, purpose. I was the cheerleader—we all were, Rabbi Ed and Rabbi Mel, too.

By second year, his moods escalated to bi-polar intensity. If he received a good grade on a Hebrew test or mastered a Talmud section he was euphoric; a bad grade or negative comment on a paper triggered doubt and defeat. In some ways, Rabbinic school was worse than prison. He was a "stranger in a strange land." He had to learn how to speak, read, write and think in Hebrew, to operate in a quieter academic universe—tough for a loud, dominating, edgy guy with a very eccentric approach to Jewish texts honed in a jail cell. He was working full time and missed more classes than anyone else when he was needed to save a life.

I wouldn't let him quit.

"What do they call a guy who graduates medical school with a "C" average? Doctor. That's right. Same goes for Rabbi."

∿

As I had anticipated, Mark's program was imparting legitimacy upon Beit T'Shuvah, in unexpected ways.

He had to spend his Rabbinic training year in Israel (like a sentence, we got it knocked down to six months), and it created a lot of turmoil and anxiety—financially, emotionally, and practically. Before he left, the Barbi Weinberg Chai Award was announced, naming an outstanding teacher of Torah, and I submitted him. The award carried a cash prize of $3,000 in addition to the honor. It would cover Mark's rent in Jerusalem and winning would give him a big send-off. I knew the story was too good—they almost had to select him—and they did. And I also knew it would put us on the map.

It was a big night for Mark and for Beit T'Shuvah, our first "coming-out" to the Big-Whigs of Jewish Federation, all our new donors, and University of Judaism. Mark's brother, the Rabbi, came down from New Jersey and his mother from Cleveland to witness his transformation and honor. It was the first time they had seen him in this light, through the eyes of his good deeds and his future goals, no longer just the failed son or the brother who'd caused so much pain and trouble. His t'shuvah was in motion. It was a boon for us. In a culture where politicians and preachers are corrupt, we're used to the good guys going bad, not the ex-cons and losers going good.

The night was proof and Mark was proof, and we were proof that our whacky, rebellious, counter-intuitive belief in change can actually work. Good can triumph over evil, boy and girl can meet and live happily ever after, helping others, "doing well by doing good."

We were becoming more "legitimate" but—thankfully—we were still as nuts and misfit-ish as ever.

~

We gleefully welcomed Federal Inmate #0742638, handcuffed and escorted by Federal Marshals. He visited us at Lake Street for three weeks, to serve his time in the Sukkah (he would first have to build) in the backyard—part of the religious-rights part of his sentencing package negotiated by Mark. We were thrilled—it was a historic first.

#0742638 was also a Chasidic Rabbi who'd laundered money for Colombian drug dealers and now needed a place where he could live in a sukkah for seven days while on leave from Federal prison. The Rabbi, leader of a large Satmer community in Los Angeles, found himself over-extended financially when the real estate bubble burst, and he was introduced to the Colombians, who were really Narcs. The surveillance video showed the Rabbi in knickers, long white silk socks and black coat and fur hat negotiating the deal with the wired drug dealers. He had no clue that he had been set up.

His attorneys asked Mark to prepare a report explaining his religious requirements, challenging the Bureau of Prisons to guarantee his religious rights, including a daily *mikva*, and his own oven to bake the Shabbos challah. The Rabbi, his wife and twelve children had never seen TV or a movie, eaten in a restaurant or read a secular book. The Bureau of Prisons insisted it would comply, and he was sentenced to 10 years in Federal prison.

At sentencing the U.S. Attorney—a Jewish woman—mocked his religious requirements: "If he's so pious, why did he consort with criminals and break the law?" To which his wife, Batya, replied, "He didn't do it on Shabbos!"

She wasn't joking.

For the three weeks between Rosh Hashanah and Sukkot, the Rabbi infused our community with Yiddishkeit and laughter. The residents helped him build and decorate the Sukkah. He taught them to bake challah. I can still see him in a white shirt and black knickers and black skull cap, kneading dough with flour on his nose, surrounded by a circle of muscled, tattooed, pierced students, braiding the dough, humming Yiddish melodies. I was in heaven.

The residents prayed and studied with him during the day, learning new songs and listening to stories. He was a youngish man and underneath the beard, *pais*, and Satmer sartorial, and he connected as one of the guys.

Then Ms. Gunderson, Federal Probation Officer arrived, asking for "inmate 0742638 living in a hut (two syllables in her southern drawl) in the yard. I'd like to see him."

"Right this way." I had to work hard not to giggle uncontrollably—as I went to find "inmate 0742638 living in a hut." Who needed TV or the movies? Every day I got to star in my very own sophisticated sitcom that not even Norman Lear could have created.

But I was sad too. I liked having him with us, and missed him when we took the Sukkah down.

I welcomed him to our "house of return" when everyone in the Jewish community—even Chabad—had turned the unusual request down and rejected him. Something drove me to live outside the lines, always eager to stretch rules and limitations. I hated bureaucracy. And rebellion? It was the quality I most admired in myself and others. For me, every rule had an exception, which I believed kindled the spirit of Beit T'Shuvah and was a crucial agent in the healing of exceptional people.

Mark made it through all his classes, exams, and Israel residency. He was ordained as a Rabbi and graduated in 2000, an event beautifully chronicled in his memoir, *The Holy Thief*. That day, I too was officially ordained with my new title: I became a Rebbetzin—the Hebrew word for Rabbi's Wife—word that is infused and elevated with expectations and responsibility.

Slowly, slowly, I was seeing I could make this thing work. I was a rebel and a Rebbetzin.

Both/and.

SACRED HOUSEKEEPING

At 55, I decided to be Bat Mitzvah-ed—in my day, girls were only confirmed. Judith HaLevy, a newly ordained Rabbi who also studied with Jonathan, prepared me and suggested that I personalize the ritual. Bat Mitzvah is a public declaration of growth and responsibility; it is a commitment to the obligations of Jewish life.

"Think of what child-like behaviors you want to leave behind."

I knew.

I opened my closet, and stared.

My dirty little secret.

Not just childish, not just a mess, cluttered and disorganized, but evidence of my fraudulence and procrastination: my lack of self care.

Acedia in action (or inaction).

To the outside world, I was a professional, a person in control. I was a powerful advocate for unlikely transformations, a healer who helped people get their lives together.

But when I opened the doors to my closets and stared in, there it was: my own darkness, my version of crazy, my shame. Shirts balled up, pants and skirts in piles on the floor, shoes lost or without mates, torn panty-hose and underpants with no elastic. My monogrammed towels from my first wedding were in tatters.

The Bat Mitzvah project became my first step toward understanding of housekeeping as something deeper than putting dresses on hangers and rolling up socks—it was a sacred act, a testament to life.

At that moment, I committed to change, or at least try my best to create habits that allowed me to live in the way I wished to live. God is both in the details and the up-keep. Everything I needed to live at peace with myself required maintenance: home, body, soul, relationships, thoughts—everything.

I took on one small disaster area at a time.

The closet project coincided with another big change—our move into a new house. I made a decision to be a grown-up: not just clean closets, but no more torn or mismatched anything. No more hoarding or cluttering. Bed, Bath & Beyond drawer organizers; shoe racks and matching towels.

This had been a lifelong struggle. For many years I just left my clothes on the floor, wherever I took them off. Many years before I had looked into my daughter's organized closet when she was 10. "Where in God's name did you learn how to do that?" All the hangers faced the same way; clothes were color-coded and in categories. My mother tightly kept herself in and put on her girdle before breakfast and hung all her clothes in garment bags. A place for everything, and everything in its place. My grandmother was also a slob, so it must skip a generation.

I thought again about Heschel's quote—*something sacred is at stake in every event.*

If God matters and I am created in the image of God, then I matter. Life matters. My actions matter.

Why bother?

Because I'm grateful for my life and my blessings.

For me, this realization changed everything—the importance of simple sacred acts—everything from maintaining the closets and drawers to making my bed. I came to believe that everyday attendance to one's physical and spiritual condition leads to a better and happier life.

Not just housekeeping: sacred housekeeping.

But it's not easy. I had witnessed many times—in myself and clients—what Jack Kornfield observes in *After the Ecstasy, the Laundry,* "the epiphanies and ah-has evaporate quickly, leaving the messes and clutter of daily life."

I stopped staring, and the work began.

～

This concept became another core principle at Beit T'Shuvah. It's relatively easy to get to a goal— but how do you stay there? The fuel of getting there is powerful: a desire to change, desperation, the will to live a different life, get different results. But staying there is tough, a different energy requiring maintenance and a kind of boredom.

Where do I find enlightenment?—Chop wood, carry water.

What is holiness?—Paying the butcher on time.

A middle-aged Dead Head came to Beit T'Shuvah because he couldn't or wouldn't get off the couch—his wife dragged him to get help. His mantra was what mine used to be: nothing matters, why bother, who cares?

The fuel of getting to goal is desire. The fuel of maintenance is commitment.   Commitment is doing the next right thing no matter how you feel. Maintenance has no rush, no payoff, no applause. Its rewards are internal. It is a statement to yourself that you matter, that caring for yourself honors God. It is a sacred obligation.

Boredom can be either blessing or curse; routine, either friend or foe. Almost every addict who has "gone out" after a period of sobriety has told me the reason was "I was bored." The maintenance of sobriety requires daily discipline and effort— same prayers, same meetings, same steps, over and over again. But I have learned to find the sameness soothing and reassuring. When I whined as a child that I was bored, my mother said that boredom was a lack of inner resources. I hated her for saying it, but now I believe she was right.

~

One day I added another important commitment—everyday I was going to make my bed.

Not to please my mother or to impress company, but to honor my life. It became a daily affirmation that I matter, what I do matters and life matters. I spend a lot of time in bed. It's my place of comfort and safety. It looks better when it's made up; it feels better when it isn't soggy and rumpled.

This realization changed everything. Making my bed always seemed to me an act of pointlessness. Why bother? It's only going to get messed up again in a few hours. Not making my bed was proof that my existential angst was correct—my statement that the inevitability of death robbed life of its meaning and therefore nothing mattered. I have now come to understand why Sloth is one of the seven deadly sins, but in those days it was a badge of honor. Slovenliness was my rebellion against a mother who had "a place for everything and everything in its place" and a society that I felt had no place for me.

I've accepted that the Sloth Monster abides within me and will always be part of me. When I try to ignore it or get mad at it, it attacks me. I have to bribe it or manipulate it or negotiate with it ... "If you'll help me honor my commitments to myself all week, we can spend the weekend in bed watching *Law & Order* re-runs... I'll treat us to goose-down pillows and 1,000-thread count new sheets."

I hated routine for many years, but now I perform my rituals and routines with missionary zeal so I don't lose my footing. These are my *mitzvot*, sacred acts. They are personal, not communal; chosen, not commanded. They remind me to be grateful to God for life: to "eat, be satisfied and bless."

I have the same conversation with myself every morning when one part of me wants to sleep an extra hour and the other one wants to get up and work out, and every night when one of me wants to drop my clothes on the floor and the other one is committed to hanging them up. Leave the dish in the sink? Wash it and put it away. It builds spiritual muscle.

All these years later, it's still a daily battle. I still get lazy and busy with distractions and acquisitions. I buy new underwear at Costco and don't bother to throw out the old. I keep things that I don't wear for over a year, a gross violation of The Organizer's Manifesto. I buy things I don't need because they're a bargain, another violation. But what's different is that now, from time to time, I force myself to face down the monster and to weed the overgrowth.

I no longer view my defects of character as evidence of my failure or as enemies to be vanquished. They are evidence only of my humanness. My daily spiritual struggle is to own them and "invite them in for tea," as Ram Dass taught.

During group sessions at Beit T'Shuvah, I began to notice that residents were adopting my evolving insights and epiphanies. A sweet and sardonic 24-year old girl who had been in eight rehabs lit up when I told my story about housekeeping as an antidote to existential despair: "I finally did my laundry after putting it off forever," she said. "I was folding the towels when I got that it's not about finding God in the Burning Bush… it's about doing your laundry. God really is in the details."

I grinned.

GOD'S AMBASSADORS

One morning I stepped over a dead body on our Lake Street steps to get to the phone ringing in my office. The Rampart Division cops asked: "Only one this time?"

Timing is everything.

The demand for our services was increasing daily, as was the gang violence around us. I knew we had to find better and bigger digs, and the timing was right to embark on expansion.

More and more Jewish families from the Westside and The Valley were discovering us—braving the ramps off the 110 to downtown, dragging their wounded loved ones up the steps or into the Shabbos tent. These were two-times-a-year people—people who only stepped in a temple on Rosh Hashana and Yom Kippur—and now they were in our tent at Friday night services on a regular basis. Their traditional networks—medical, legal, institutional—were not able to help them. Even the blessed among us are not immune. We were the last stop. They were both ashamed and relieved to meet people they knew or knew of, under our tent.

It was underground. A buzz in the zeitgeist. Secretive. It's hard to imagine that there was a time when rehab and 12 steps weren't in the popular culture, and shows like *Intervention* and *Addicted* and *Hoarders* and *Celebrity Rehab* didn't exist yet. We weren't yet at the 99th monkey phenomena, where recognition spreads like a virus after the first cluster "catches it." Parents with addicted kids thought they were the only one, and kept their shame a secret. They were hardworking, traditional Jewish parents with high expectations of themselves, their children, the world, and others—were now hurt, ashamed, blind-sided, and horrified by their loved one's exceptional falls and the wreckage that one broken family member can create.

These children of Jewish fairy-tale couples weren't becoming the princes and princesses they were supposed to in the stories: they were turning into *shondas*—to themselves and others. Their parents expected to be attending Harvard graduation, not standing in the Visitors line at County Jail.

I witnessed movers and shakers and Kings of industry crumble, confused that forces beyond them had abducted the children whose teeth had once been perfectly straightened by the best orthodontists, and who were now meth addicts spinning like whackos, and sleeping with rats. Nothing they had done or knew prepared them for this or for their love and generosity being repaid with stealth and rape of trust and violence. "We gave him everything; how could this happen?"

People were practically spilling out of our tent's Friday night services. We didn't have enough beds for all who called. And the intensifying violence around us on Lake Street was starting to really concern me. It was time to move. Where? How? Who would help us?

Need wasn't a mystery, nor was filling it.

One night I spotted Annette Shapiro walking into our tent for services. <u>The</u> Annette Shapiro.

I looked at Mark. "Oh my God—What's she doing here?

In his book, *The Tipping Point*, Malcolm Gladwell introduces a woman named Lois Cohen, a person of many connecting circles, whose opinion influences others and who can make things happen. In the Los Angeles Jewish Community, that person is Annette Shapiro, a "professional volunteer."

Later Annette called me and explained why she came. She was being installed as President of the Jewish Community Foundation at the Skirball Museum, and since the Foundation helped open the Beit T'Shuvah Women's House, she wanted me and a few of the residents to speak at her dinner "so the members can see their dollars at work."

In the non-profit world this event was equivalent to opening on Broadway or debuting at Carnegie Hall. The Jewish Community Foundation manages millions of dollars and its Board members are all powerful, wealthy business and professional leaders and philanthropists.

I brought Lola to the dinner—a 42 year old child of Holocaust survivors. She had progressed from a functional heroin user who was a working paralegal to a street hooker. We had advocated for her with the Court and she had been sentenced to Beit T'Shuvah for one year.

"They got me out on a Friday and that night," Lola says. "I said the Shema under the tent with my Jewish brothers and sisters... I hadn't prayed in 20 years. I also said Kaddish for my mother... I was too strung out to be at her funeral and I was an only child..."

I heard a few people catch their breath and saw some wipe their eyes. "I want all of you to know that your efforts saved my life."

Annette started the applause and they all stood and clapped from the soul, reluctant to sit down. All their stereotypes cracked apart as a Jewish junkie and prostitute—from a good family, Holocaust survivors ("for God's sake!")—told her story. This controlled, bottom-line, type-A crowd were grateful to be touched in a place they thought they had lost. They were soul struck! Raw emotion. They were all givers and were seeing that their giving actually helps.

At the beginning of the evening I believed I was a beggar. When I left I knew I was a merchant in a fair trade agreement. I give them Hope; they give me Money. I saw the vision: together we would move Beit T'Shuvah out of the barrio to the Westside, where we belonged.

I didn't know exactly how or when, but I knew it would happen.

∼

Annette calls a month later. "People are still thanking me for the installation, telling me how moved they were," she says.

She halts. There's something else. I wait.

"We never think it will happen to us, you know..."

She tells me that her granddaughter just called from jail. She and her husband, Leonard, had to have her arrested. She thinks what she is telling me is unique. It is not. It's why we need three buildings and a major Capital Campaign.

It's why we need her.

"She stole our checks and forged them. We had to press charges... we couldn't even look at one another as they led her away in handcuffs... Calling you is the last thing I will ever do for her and I don't want her to know I called. She'll go to Court in a few days for commercial burglary. I'm only asking you to visit her and see if she wants help, if she's not right for you, don't take her just because of us—please."

I get her booking number. I tell her I'll go see her tomorrow, and if she wants help, Mark and I will be in Court. I remind her that her granddaughter and my husband have a lot in common—he forged checks too.

I hung up the phone and shook my head in awe. I've said it and heard it, but, could this really be the hand of God? Was this also part of the miracle started in Janet Levy's office?

There are several million Jews in Los Angeles, many of them wealthy, but there is only one Annette Shapiro. Annette Shapiro needs my help and I need hers. Annette's blessing will advance our visibility and credibility exponentially—she's the Charity trend-setter. People will be scalping tickets to our Steps to Recovery Ball next year. Addicts will be IN... We'll fix her granddaughter and we'll honor Annette and Leonard, and Erin will present the award! (And it happened just like that, years later).

This is the mercenary fact: I can't help Annette's granddaughter or anyone without funds. And since we are a "faith-based" institution and can't receive government funds, we rely on private donors, foundations, the Jewish Community.

And that has become part of the Beit T'Shuvah culture too—when you can, what you can, you give.

I tell Mark he needs to go visit "a paperhanger in Sybil Brand... who happens to be Annette Shapiro's granddaughter...I think you're the one to pay her a visit... shock the shit out of her, but don't blow it."

Mark gets the judge to sentence Erin to Beit T'Shuvah for one year, along with a promise to pay restitution to the bank and spiritual amends to her grandparents. He closed with his own story of redemption. Her grandparents were not there.

Erin came to us for treatment, for compulsive lying and stealing, and like all of our residents, had a story. She turned her hurt into rage, replacing the love she had lost with goods, stealing them to even the score. She realized that stealing from her grandparents, "the only people who always loved me," was a violent act, equivalent to rape. "I raped their trust..." she tells me. She misses them and wants to seek forgiveness. A month later I call Annette and ask her if she and Leonard are ready to listen to Erin's amends.

The Shapiros knock on the door ten minutes ahead of the scheduled meeting. Was the terror on their frozen faces from parking their Jaguar on this gang-infested street or coming face-to-face with their granddaughter? They had not seen her since the day she was led away in handcuffs.

We sit in a small circle. I see tears well up in both their eyes. I am watching a silent Greek tragedy of love and betrayal, a passion play of Good and Evil.

I had seen it before.

I know why she ripped them off—because she knew they loved her. Addicts often abuse the people closest to them—they have easy access and they bank on escaping consequences. It's survival for them.

"*Pressing charges took real courage,*" I say. "*One day, if we're successful and she 'gets it' she'll thank you, I promise.*"
"*Tough love is tough,*" Leonard states matter of factly.

They want to bolt, but they don't.

"*Forgiveness is a process. It takes time and effort to restore trust,*" I tell them. "*You'll keep hearing my husband say that t'shuvah is not just 'I'm sorry,' it's having a plan not to repeat the same behavior. He also says that when the torn fabric of the relationship has been re-stitched, the fabric will be stronger.*"

Then I address Erin. "*Take a good look at the hurt in their eyes. It's time for you to realize that you're not entitled to hurt others just because you've been hurt.*"

And then I say the contradiction that is a truth: "*Victims are the worst victimizers.*"

Erin apologizes, they discuss what happened and ask why. She asks for forgiveness and for them to come for services. They're not ready but they'll stay in touch with me. I watch as the older Shapiros walk out, following them down the street from the safety of the porch.

I feel like a voyeur, a witness to raw, undefended intimacy.

~

Annette "adopted" me, Mark and Beit T'Shuvah, and invited us into her family. We invited her into the Beit T'Shuvah family. As my mother/mentor, she groomed me for leadership. She arranged for a dentist to fix my disappearing teeth. She introduced me to her country club friends and other non-profit execs. I paid attention—how they dressed and interacted with each other and me. I figured out my "place"—not friend, not employee, not peer;

more like a daughter who wanted their help and was grateful for their suggestions.

In 1999 Annette nominated me for the Visions in Philanthropy Award sponsored by the Jewish Community Foundation and Freeman, Freeman & Smiley law firm. They all came to "kvell" as I accepted the award and was promoted from an Idealist Dreamer to a Visionary.

Annette also became the sparkplug that ignited our first Capital Campaign, convincing Warren Breslow (first Board President) and a few other believers that we could raise $5,000,000 bucks to move to the Westside.

Raising the money was easy compared to the resistance of the Homeowners Associations that didn't want us in their backyard, who fought our conditional use permits. Eventually Warren found a board and care that was inhabited by "homeless" mentally ill who threw shit out the windows and were definitely bringing down property values. Our Jewish addicts looked good in comparison.

The dedication of the Warren & Elaine Breslow, Jonah Goldrich, Saul Kest Beit T'Shuvah was attended by over 300 "machers" and politicos in November 1999. The almost-ordained Mark Borovitz introduced Rabbi Ed Feinstein, who set the tone when the power went out… "God wants us to know we don't have to be perfect!"

I "came out" on the National Scene at the Lion of Judah conference in Washington, D.C. Annette took me and introduced me to all the Big Lions from every city—women who give at least $25,000 to Jewish Federations. While we were in Washington, I arranged for us to visit Jim Towey, the Director of the Office of Faith-Based and Community Initiatives. We made an instant connection, despite his being a G.W. Bush appointee. He had a mezuzah on his door and several books by Rabbi Abraham Joshua Heschel, his favorite theologian. I told him my husband also loved Heschel and I gave him a copy of *The Holy Thief*, Mark's book. We talked about Beit T'Shuvah, addiction and faith-based recovery and agreed on everything. This was truly a miracle!

"You'll be hearing from me," he said, as he kissed us good-bye.

FAITH-BASED

I'm sitting in my office, reading in my favorite chair. We completed the Capital Campaign, and we're in the Westside building. The receptionist beeps.

"The White House! It's the White House!"

For years I'd said: "No interruptions unless it's the White House," as a joke, and I think it's a joke. But it is the White House. Jim Towey, President George Bush's Director of Faith-Based and Community Initiatives, would be coming to visit. He was looking for a model faith-based program to feature at the National Conference in D.C.

The day came, and I waited in the lobby, as anxious as a teenager on Prom night. He walked in and hugged me, trailed by a lone reporter from a local station. I took him first to the Sanctuary, explaining the Beit T'Shuvah story told by the stained glass windows, focusing on the image of the Torah surrounded by barbed wire.

I opened the ark and showed him the Torah that had been rescued from the Holocaust and restored by the Memorial Scrolls Trust in London, which our first Board had donated to us at a special event in 1990.

"A recovered Torah for recovering addicts," I said.

We walked through the dining room where residents were lining up for breakfast, catching the excitement of a special visitor. They loved showing me off and bragging about Beit T'Shuvah... *This place saved my life; I've been in ten other rehabs; do you know the President?*

I took him to the Board Room where Mark, the staff, Warren Breslow, and four residents and alumni were assembled around the conference table. Everyone shared, including Jim, who asked pointed questions about the relationship between Judaism and AA and what the turning point had been for each of them.

"I'm Roger. I'm 22 years old. I grew up in Bloomfield Hills, Michigan, a wealthy suburb of Detroit, in a wonderful family where everything looked good on the outside... it was a Jewish family, but not a Jewish home... I wanted my father to be proud of me, so I told him everything I thought he wanted to hear... but inside I was confused and I felt like an alien, like I'd never measure up to him... I started getting high at around 11, still getting good grades, living a double life—lying, stealing, conning everybody including myself. It all fell apart my first semester in college, and I've been in one rehab after another since then..."

Then Jen spoke: "I thought I was fat and ugly and stupid and I didn't fit in with the blond, popular Melissas and Jessicas or get asked out by the doctors-to-be. So I went the other way, into the hell of methamphetamines and crime and violence. These people found me in jail a year and a half ago, went to Court for me....

my boyfriend had chopped off my hair and literally knocked out all my teeth in a jealous rage. I was facing State Prison for drug sales, my family was too ashamed to come visit me…Harriet and the Rabbi rescued me… They came to Court, took me into their spiritual home here and loved me until I could love myself. They even found a dentist who replaced my teeth—pro bono… Now I work here as an assistant counselor and I'm enrolled at UCLA extension to get my credential in alcohol and drug counseling…"

And on and on around the table.

True stories.

Real lives.

After each spoke, Jim looked at us: "I visit a lot of these places and have been around many faith-based communities, and I know beyond a shadow of doubt that God dwells in this holy place."

Mark seized his cue: "*Kodesh Barechu*, Master of the Universe, thank you for opening our hearts, for the power to heal the broken hearted and connect us to one another and to you!"

"I'll be sure to tell the President about Beit T'Shuvah," Jim promised as he left, and in December of 2003, we received a handwritten letter and a personal check for $1,000 from George and Laura Bush:

> *Dear Harriet and Rabbi Borovitz: My friend, Jim Towey, told me of the wonderful work that you and your team are doing at Beit T'Shuvah. Laura and I are thankful for your compassion and generous spirit.*
> *May God continue to bless your efforts.*
> *Sincerely,*
> *George W. Bush*

We were invited to appear on the dais with the President at two conferences focused on his Faith Based and Access to Recovery initiatives. Mark escorted him into the auditorium, and the President introduced Mark and himself as "two old drunks who found God."

He said: "The government wants to stand side-by-side with people of faith who work to change people's lives. It's not fair for the government to discriminate against a program because there's a Rabbi on the Board, a cross on the wall, or a crescent on the door... It makes no sense, if you're a faith-based program, not to practice your faith if you want Federal money."

I jumped up as he finished and clapped until my palms hurt. All around the country, people saw me clapping and the President embracing Mark on CNN and called to tell us. Some of them called us traitors: "How could you let yourself be used by him? How could you sit in the same room with that man?" Talk about both/and. I liked him and felt honored to be kissed by the President of the United States. I still hated his politics. *The Washington Post*, the next morning, had a front-page picture of Rabbi Mark Borovitz of Beit T'Shuvah with President Bush. I wondered if our socialist fathers were turning over in their graves.

When we got back to Los Angeles, Mark wrote a check to the Bush campaign for $100 and to the Kerry campaign for $1,000.

~

The naysayers won, and this great, visionary program fell apart. I wrote a very long "love" letter to President George Bush that I never sent. Here's an excerpt that expresses my sincere and still-active wish about Faith Based programs and funding:

...In a true Messianic age you wouldn't have had to by-pass Congress to implement the faith-based initiatives. A bipartisan Congress, presented with empirical evidence that spirituality is the only vitamin that cures the scurvy of addiction in all its forms, would embrace it as a solution and not resist it as a threat to the separation of church and state or a violation of equal opportunity employment. You and I know the truth of this. I applaud your courage in activating "Access to Recovery" by Executive Order. Kol HaKvod to you. Your God and my God probably still belong to different theological parties, but we agree wholeheartedly that faith in God restores the soul and resurrects the spirit.
Sincerely,
Harriet

Faith-based became a real conundrum. It didn't entitle us to government money because of First Amendment separation of church and state requirements. We were eligible to apply for Federal funds, but because we mandated Torah study and Shabbat services, we didn't meet charitable choice rules... You can only receive faith-based funding if you take out the faith part.

Because faith-based was so linked to G.W. it worked against us with a number of donors and foundations. I learned fast how uncomfortable people could be when I was preparing a grant proposal to pay off our mortgage and endow Beit T'Shuvah. The Rabbi of the Foundation called me after reading the first draft:

"Take out all references to Faith-Based or Judaism."

"Huh? That's what we do—that's who we are."

"We know your wonderful work, Harriet, and we're all very proud of you. These trustees on our Board are Wall Street guys who happen to have been born Jewish. They hate Faith-based.

They give lip service to Judaism but they come to Temple twice a year, if that. They view religion as superstition, a sign of naiveté or stupidity. They want evidence-based best practices stuff."

The irony of my stance didn't escape me. I believed in Separation of Church and State. I had been them and would still be if not for Beit T'Shuvah—religion is the opiate of the masses; people of faith were delusional. The Faith-based people were my sworn enemies: Right Wing, self-righteous, hypocritical morons. And in other people's eyes I had become them: The Enemy, destroyer of rational, scientific solutions.

I struggled to find the words to convince the Rabbi that faith in a Power greater than oneself was necessary in order to stay sober. The addict has to learn how to live from within and stop seeking external solutions to internal discomfort…

"As a matter of fact, Rabbi, this is true of all people. The psychology of Judaism is brilliant in teaching us how to overcome shame and the addictive pursuit of 'Golden Calves.'"

… I'm teaching the Rabbi about Judaism!!!

He understood. He understood better than I did.

"Your goal is not to enlighten them, Harriet. Your goal is to lighten their assets by $2,000,000 so you can continue to heal people your way."

I stood still. Questions came at me. Am I selling out if I shut up and take their money? Is this the beginning of the erosion of my integrity? My husband the Rabbi was clear: "*Nem the gelt*, take the money. The Talmud teaches you have to speak to people in a way they can hear."

"Two million dollars is a lot of money. Saves a lot of souls..."

"If I'm going to be a hooker, at least I ain't no 2 dollar whore!" I joked.

Mark and I continue to preach our Jewish Gospel. Torah is the Big Book of Jewish recovery from human broken-ness. We believe if you can see yourself in every Parsha it is the Path to Shalem (wholeness) and Shalom (Peace of Mind).

Our Shabbos and Holiday services attract increasing numbers of people who either suffered through other services or left Jewish life altogether. They love the fun and spontaneity, the connection with others, the music that rocks their souls and the witnessing of the Power of Redemption. They tell us often, "If it had been like this, I never would have left!" We hear it all the time as more and more seekers of a meaningful spiritual connection (Jews and non-Jews) "discover" us. Their gratitude and excitement for not being bored both saddens and excites me. We really have something they want. That's the good news. The bad news is: why haven't they found it anyplace else?

Mark and I still struggle to change the common misconception held by some "real" clergy and congregations that our "brand" of worship works only for addicts!

THE PLACE OF PING

The Talmud attributes our uniqueness to the Divine. Each of us is imprinted with a kaleidoscope of divine particles that shape our essence and urge us to discover and claim our authentic, original selves. God created man *Tzelem Elohim*, in the image of God, and it's the life's work of every human being to gather all of these particles, (the ones we like and the ones we don't like) and to construct a life that expresses all of us. It is a pilgrimage each of us must make to wholeness, a journey to our personal Holy Soul.

That is the real work of Beit T'Shuvah—helping lost souls find the image of God that is his or hers. And as long as we're hooked on external approval we're not free to express our own *tzelem Elohim*.

The path to the place of "ping" is a process of trying on and discarding the false selves (the ones that thud like lead glass), which we have created in order to meet the expectations of our families and our culture. They are the conditioned responses and social roles in which we clothe ourselves in order to fit in and to win the acceptance and admiration of others.

As long as other people have the power of God over you, you are not free to be you.

~

A man asks a Rabbi if he can study the Kabbalah, so he can learn the mysteries of the universe. The Rabbi asks him: When people flatter you, my son, do you feel good? And when they criticize you, do you feel bad? Yes, Rabbi, of course I do. Then go away; you're not ready to study the mysteries of the universe.

I recognized it in myself.

I knew that this meant that to connect to the Divine, to be free to study the mysteries of the universe, you have to be a God Pleaser, not a People Pleaser. I had been a compulsive People Pleaser.

I wanted to be a God pleaser.

The shift from false to authentic, from lead glass to crystal begins with looking within, it's an inside job: the inner and outer person is the same and we ping like crystal. *In her book The Gifts of Imperfection*, Brené Brown distinguishes between fitting in and belonging. Fitting in almost always requires denying or silencing parts of yourself. Belonging welcomes all of you. I am proud to be called Queen of the Mis-Fits.

Many of our clients—especially those with everything to live for and everything to lose—are hooked on expectations, external confirmations and approval. Failing to find it, they seek relief in substances, activities, possessions and bad friends and romances. They substitute self-pity for self-worth, and confuse self-worth with net worth. They accept their conditioning as their authentic self.

The Expect a Miracle Lady (who changed my life) practiced Religious Science. The biblical phrase—"As a man thinketh in his heart, so is he,"—is their basic belief. The message was clear and simple: change your thoughts, change your life; what you can conceive and believe, you can achieve. Janet's admonition to "Pay attention" had guided me to my mission—what other miracles awaited me? The basic idea was that thoughts are living things and I could bring into my life that which I think most about. Negative or positive.

My value is not comparative or conditional. It is my birthright only. It's not easy to hold on to this power. The claws of conditioning dig deep and when I allow someone to make me feel lousy about myself or question my worth, I try not to hang out too long in that place.

When I was young, I was totally "hooked" on approval. My happiness and self-worth were dependent on attention, flattery, and other people's opinions of me, particularly boys. And it made me unhappy, empty, and anxious. I could never be thin enough or smart enough or pretty enough to matter. No matter how hard I worked at it, I was always a little bit "off".

I took on a challenge to define and clarify what I really thought, disconnected from the conditioned, pre-packaged expectations of society or the flattery and criticism of others or the myths of happiness and perfection, to choose my reactions. This became a kind of sacred housekeeping too—a cleaning up of thoughts.

If I was alone on a Saturday night or New Year's Eve, Thanksgiving or my birthday, or any holiday for that matter, I felt the despair of rejection and non-existence. On week nights or non-holidays, I was content to be by myself, reading a book. I became a detective, seeking clues to conditioned reactions or authentic feelings.

Thanksgiving was my first success. I made it just another Thursday. It set me free to go to the movies by myself and to enjoy the day without responsibilities, crowds, or forced family dinners. New Year's Eve became December 31 and went from nightmare to vacation—I stayed home, crawled under the covers, and got lost in the latest True Crime. When I woke up it was January of the next year, another day. No resolutions, party hats, or disappointment.

My Birthday—December 29—between Christmas and New Year's was always fraught and forgotten. I finally figured out how to celebrate by giving myself all the things I enjoy. No more hating all the people who didn't buy me the things I really wanted. I thank my mother for giving me life and I commit to another year of taking good care of myself.

I am also blessed to have a husband who knows my soul and finds a gift I really want but am too cheap to buy. One year he got me a trainer—who made me feel young and powerful. Most recently he picked out a silver sequined Coach handbag that is me, that I was too cheap to ever buy for myself.

February 14th?

Just another day.

~

Every day I see evidence that we are teaching our children to thud, not to ping.

In 2011, a 14-year old boy bolted from an after-school baseball game in Santa Monica, ran to a nearby hotel, and jumped to his death from the 10th floor as his classmates watched in horror. In one of the local papers another student said: "I've known him since mid-sixth grade... and ever since then he's been by far the happiest guy I've ever met in my life"

It didn't make CNN, but it rocked our world here in LA.

His Rabbi expressed the communal shock in an interview: "He was certainly not the kind of person you would expect to have these feelings... Something went horribly, horribly wrong."

He was bright, upbeat and dependable and gave no indication he was seriously troubled. He was popular, good in sports, showed no signs of distress. It was without warning.

Something went horribly wrong—but what?

I didn't know him or the family, and can't say specifically, but I have seen hundreds and hundreds of promising young people who come to us with a story that's some version of happiest-guy/girl types: prettiest/handsomest, smartest, athletic star, etc... And then seemingly without warning, he/she is in jail, or smashing their fists in the walls, or crashing the car, or stealing, or in ICU, overdosed, or under-fed. They break under the weight of their parent's expectations, tired of being "golden children."

Doug Rosen is the Director of our Partners in Prevention Program, heading up a team of recovering Jewish addicts who tell their stories to middle and high school kids and parents in schools, camps, and synagogues around the country. When they sit down with these teens, they hear the truth about the pressure they feel to "fit in," to be the best at everything and to feel happy all the time.

He gets it.

Doug was the quintessential Beverly Hills kid, and then became an up-and-coming young producer. He'd started smoking pot regularly early in high school when his parents split up, and then progressed to harder drugs. When he was arrested, he was burning through $200 a day in heroin, cocaine, and some crystal meth. Doug's rock bottom came when he destroyed his car, lost his girlfriend and his cool job, and was arrested for stealing underwear at Nordstroms when he was high on speedballs. He arrived at Beit T'Shuvah directly from jail.

He begins with a re-telling of his own experience of the family dinner table conversation:

How do you feel? (anxious parent)
Fine. (monosyllabic teen)
What did you learn in school?
Nothing.

The kids around the country also answer, fine. They admit that they feel their parents don't really want to hear the truth, or will freak out and interrogate them, or they'll lose privileges. They learn how to "play the game"—at home and at school, and they know that as long as they look okay on the outside and get good grades, their secrets are safe because they know their parents don't want to know. Overlooked by looking good.

They've done everything they were supposed to do and more, and they still feel empty inside. They perform without passion and strive without purpose. True or not, perfect kids feel that they aren't allowed to have doubts and fears or problems. The "best and the brightest" suffer, but aren't supposed to.

And after I read about the 14 year old boy's suicide, I wondered: if all everyone wanted was for him to be his happy self, and if he wasn't, did he feel he was letting them down? Was he the carrier of his parents' and grandparents' vision of perfection? Did his spirit get profoundly crushed by these seemingly ordinary, benign expectations?

~

Back in the 1980's, Warren and Elaine Breslow didn't have many reference points when their son Corey spun out irrevocably. They were self-made, wealthy, successful people. Elaine came out publicly at a conference in 1988, called The Not-So-Secret-Secret of Addiction in the Jewish Community. Mark and I introduced ourselves after her key-note speech in which she "came out" as a Princess who did not "live happily ever after" when she discovered her elder son smoking pot and sniffing glue at the age of 10. They became our friends, and core to everything we have done and become.

We lost Elaine in 2011, and we named the Family program after her.

Back then, she stood on the stage and was my hero as she exploded the myth of The Perfect Jewish Family. They had access to everything money could buy (including the best medical treatment); cost was no object, but no one knew how to help them with Corey's drug problem—it doesn't happen to Jewish kids!

They struggled privately in shame and isolation through years of psychiatrists, mental hospitals and expensive 28-day rehabs; spent many nights pretending sleep, waiting for the phone call or the door bell that would tell them that Corey was dead or in jail. One day it came. Instead of killing herself, Elaine returned to school to become an alcohol and drug counselor in order to better cope, herself, and to use her experience to help others. Both she and Warren became core to Beit T'Shuvah, and with their story out there, a lamp was lit for the "nice Jewish families": if it could happen to the Breslows—who seemed like them—and they could speak about it, maybe it wasn't such a *shondah* after all.

Two decades after Elaine spoke, it's the same archetypal story, only the names and addresses change. American Jewish families, who have fulfilled the ancestral dream of the "Goldena medina," are baffled by their children's refusal to grab the baton, do better than they did, or act responsibly with the opportunities and resources they are given.

He/She is our brightest, the sweetest… where did we go wrong? … We gave him/her everything … he/she could have been anything he/she wanted to be— what happened?

Ambition and "effort-er" muscles become atrophied by being given too much, too soon. Self-esteem is stunted by feeling both entitlement and inadequacy, a losing combination. The upward mobility ladder is toppling. Kids know they never will be as rich or powerful as their parents and can only compete by not wanting what they had or refusing to become who they wanted them to be, because—deep down—they felt that they never would or could measure up.

Biblical rivalries have been passed down *l'dor v'dor,* from generation to generation. Over the years at Beit T'Shuvah, I have heard from both mothers and fathers that if their siblings (or neighbor) knew the truth of their shame, they would gloat. If their parents or grandparents found out he/she had failed out of college and was in rehab they would drop dead. What will the neighbors think? … You don't air your dirty linen in public… are messages of shame, zero tolerance of anything other than the Perfect Picture.

I have taken the same hysterical call from countless mothers: "I know he's only a level one; the Court says he can't leave; he just got out of jail; everyone will be drinking … but his sister/ brother's wedding, Bar/Bat Mitzvah, his grandparents' 50th anniversary—he has to be in the pictures. When we look at the album later and he smiles at us and looks normal, we can forget for a moment that she's a drug addict, living proof of our failure as parents, evidence of our shame.

I wanted that picture too: we all do. Thank God for Photoshop!

~

I am witness to the constantly imploding myth of perfection and the way it can ravage a soul, a family, the future.

Our Jewish God only demands that we own our flaws, make amends to those we have harmed as a result, and return to battle. All you have to do to please God is to be your true self (bad and good) and learn how to do more good deeds than bad ones. You don't have to get all "A's" or win first prize or be tall, thin and gorgeous, rich and powerful. Doesn't matter where you live or what you drive or where you vacation or where your children go to school or if your caterer or trainer is on the "A" list. Doesn't matter if you're famous or gifted or charismatic.

If you feel that you're living a double life or trading truth for acceptance, that's where the emptiness and sense of futility comes in. And that's why you find substances and activities to numb the despair of lifelessness.

Every person who has come to us has a story of how they lost themselves. And if they make it, how they got found as well, and found the "self" that is unique and true.

As Beit T'Shuvah's program evolved, we began to see a pattern. That those who found that "ping," their authentic self, who found something they loved to do and work on, had a greater success at sobriety. We changed our motto and mission from helping heal addiction, to helping people recover their passion and discover their purpose.

Rachel, our cantor, is an example of transformation—from paralyzing unrealistic expectations of herself, to self realization. When I hear her sing it's hard to believe the gift of the exquisite song of her soul might have been silenced. As she wrote of her journey:

> *I came to Beit T'Shuvah and, ultimately, Harriet's office, a broken individual. I was an expert on internalizing the world's expectations of me (which were often very distorted in my head) and then using them as constant "proof" to myself that I was a failure in life after I made mistakes. My family, my teachers, you name it…there were so many voices in my head constantly telling me how I was wrong. It seemed that the only expectations I was unaware of were my own. I was a perfectionist in the most self-destructive way and cycled through my life as if I could never measure up to "my potential"—a concept I also managed to form from comparing myself to others, and never independently evaluating myself… I had absolutely no grasp on who I really was as an individual, and that was basically my disease. It was no single exchange or epiphany-like moment, but several small-yet-monumental realizations… Starting with "I matter." I transformed from a fragmented soul into a symbiotic spirit; a shattered girl into a grown woman aware of herself and knowing what exactly she had to offer to the world.*

We are both grateful that she chose to come to Beit T'Shuvah instead of killing herself.

John Sullivan's story has a similar framework—from lost soul with a heroin habit and 20 convictions, to a purpose and passion he didn't even know existed. In excerpts from an article he published in BTS Magazine:

My story started with me in handcuffs and has ended with me starting BTS Communications. Truly amazing…I had become a two-time loser. I was one step closer to a life trapped in the revolving doors of addiction and the justice system. But I had also surrendered and turned my will and my life over to God and God definitely had taken over… I really believed I never had to be shackled again… What I have done is embarked on an amazing journey of finding my passion and discovering my purpose. What I have done is embarked on an amazing journey of finding my passion and discovering my purpose…

I was not the first to notice my talent for graphic design and the whole social media thing. No, it was Rabbi and Harriet, especially Rabbi. He managed to figure out what I should pursue. Following his direction, I enrolled in school, learned all the crazy software. It paid off and before I knew it I was working for Beit T'Shuvah doing all the graphic design stuff and giving everything a fresh, modern feel. I dabbled with Facebook and Twitter and YouTube for Beit T'Shuvah and to my amazement I was able to get that to start working as well. Well, Rabbi and Harriet in their infinite wisdom could see this whole thing a lot better than I and they knew the next step…

I view Judaism as core to a program of recovery for the addiction to perfection as well. All of our heroes are imperfect. The Torah is the story of our people's struggle to submit their will to God's Will, to act themselves into right thinking and being. Over and over they forget God's directions, lose faith and gratitude and build "golden calves" to fill the hole of their separation from God. We are still forgetting, and building golden calves and "golden children," to whom we pray for "happily ever after."

Just as I had confused American Jewish culture with Judaism, so have most of our families. The teachings of Judaism are clear: Be who you are, don't compare yourself to anyone. Your value is a birthright. You will make mistakes and you can always return. We are passing down a diluted message and our children are becoming deaf to us.

As Reb Zusya told his disciples: "When I go before God, he won't ask me, "Zusya, why were you not more like Moses?" If He asks, "Why were you not more like Zusya?" woe unto me."

This is the message our children need to hear: Be you, not me or even who I want you to be.

THE FAIR IS IN POMONA

Dear New Resident of Beit T'Shuvah:

A bed opened up.

You are male or female, young or old, rich or poor. But if you can't pay, we won't turn you away.

Your parents or your spouse or your children or your friends might've dropped you off and left, in tears. This is your last chance they shout. They might mean it, maybe not. You will probably test it.

But for now, you go to intake.

You are angry. You are in trouble. You are in pain.

You have no idea what's happening.

Life sucks. We suck.

It sucks.

It really sucks.

All of it.

When you come to my office to talk to me, to tell me your story (you have one, everyone who breaks apart does), I tell you it's fucked. Just like that.

I do it deliberately. I want to shock you so you'll re-evaluate your perceptions. I'm an old-lady and a CEO and I have done a thousand wilder, weirder things than you will ever know. As has my husband, The Rabbi, who will also at some point be screaming some version of you're fucked, fuck you, you're a fucking prick, it's fucked, they're fucked, who the fuck...??? etc, etc... etc... In the future, that will probably make you smile. Not yet though.

I get it.

We get it.

You'll get that soon too.

My qualification to be your life teacher is I have been where you are.

I've seen it all. I know your torment, your war against yourself. I have battle-hardened experience and I still struggle every day.

And I have learned how to live an integrated life.

You will too.

You are sure that whatever you're addicted to is the only thing that will relieve the misery of your emptiness, the hole that aches. Without (fill in your own blanks) drugs, alcohol, gambling, sex, food, money, power and prestige... there is no reason to get up in the morning.

You will see eventually that the agenda is to hand you back your life and teach you how to be You, the authentic you, to stop comparing yourself to others and judging your worth comparatively and conditionally.

 I can help you find the ammunition to tame your self-defeating demons, your "What's the point?" "Why bother?" "Fuck it!" voice that "crouches at your door."

I don't give a shit about your tattoos, piercings, hair styles, costumes or kashrut. They are only props you used when your spirit was subdued. You don't yet understand that rebellion is not freedom: you have merely conformed to different masters.

We will bombard you with alternative highs and rushes—surfing, singing, drama, art, writing, cooking, joining the choir or band. You might run the marathon or play golf or do yoga. We will teach you how to have fun in sobriety—dancing, sports, concerts. We will allow you to have relationships and will be there every step of the way, so you can learn how to draw on the power of love to better regulate your own reactions and emotions. You will learn patience, acceptance and tolerance in relationship with one another.

You will have a daily and weekly schedule that is an integrative treatment model: Jewish wisdom and spirit, addiction counseling and 12 Step recovery, and therapy of one kind or another. Like every resident you will have a team—a counselor, vocational counselor, spiritual counselor and therapist. You will become part of the Beit T'Shuvah culture and learn that it's an individual program too. What's good for one may not be good for another. We strive to do as we say and to be transparent. Right is not determined by rank or identity by role. Each of us has a job to do but all souls are equal. We honor one another's vulnerabilities and do not use them to manipulate or harm one another (most of the time) we strive to place principles before personalities and to Be the Change we want for you.

Some days you will hate me.

Us.

Yourself.

Everybody.

You will want to leave.

You will want to use again, and you might.

But if you don't, one day you will start to feel better.

Alive again, in fact.

Connection to this community will become a stronger connection than connection to your dope dealer. And ultimately we help you frame your life by connection to a Higher and Eternal truth that governs your choices and provides a road map for the journey. And then back to the things and people who are important to you.

You will know that we care about helping you find the "Song of your Soul," reviving your shrunken spirit, igniting your passion for life and discovering your life's purpose.

You will see that we mean it and believe it when we say that Judaism teaches that everyone has a place in the world, the world is incomplete without you: you matter, everyone matters.   You will come to feel responsible to your unique place, and sense more of the obligation to "repair your corner of the world."

You will hear us say: Everyone has a purpose. It will take a while to believe it.

You feel hopeless, lost, ashamed. You will feel you have fallen too far, failed too hard to ever come back, or have the right to ever be forgiven.

And we will show you the divine workings of t'shuvah, of redemption and return.

This mind-set of perfection is totally contrary to Jewish teaching.   Judaism is a spirituality rooted in acceptance of human imperfection.   We are imperfect by Divine design with both animal and Divine inclinations—neither good nor evil, but endowed with both free will and the power to harness the energy of evil and to choose good.   We become good when we admit and take responsibility for our evil inclinations and take contrary action no matter what we feel! Judaism is a religion of deeds, not creeds; we are judged by our actions, not our intentions. Our traits all come from God and are not intrinsically good or evil.   They are human, and our challenge as humans is to know ourselves and heal the parts (traits) that are out of proper measure.

You will be exhausted that first week, but you will stand up at your first Shabbat services where you and the other new residents will be introduced by name, to take your place here, and be welcomed—and you will look out at the tribe welcoming you in.

Now they are strangers.

But soon they will be your community, and you will find the connection you crave.

Hope will replace dope.

Recovery is a very tough journey. It's painful—physically, mentally, spiritually. It's the darkest moments, the toughest demons, the most hopeless abject failures faced.

The only requirement is that you stay on the journey.

You will say: life isn't fair, and then you die.

And I will tell you I used to believe that too. But now, when I hear _it_ (life, the pain, the process, the stuff, all of it…) *isn't fair,* I say: "Fair? The fair is in Pomona."

So just hang on.

Amen.

LOVE IS NOT A FEELING

Mark arrived at my apartment at 12:30 a.m. one March night in the late 1980's with everything he owned stuffed in a laundry bag, just released from his half-way house.

"Hi, Honey, I'm home."

I let him in.

We have made our home together ever since.

Was I nuts?

Harriet—where are your instincts? I could hear my mother say, just like she did when I'd gotten in trouble with the door man drug dealer who threatened to kill me.

My instincts?

Was I doing the same thing I had always done, expecting different results? Mark was 14 years younger. Would everyone assume I was just his meal ticket, providing "three hots and a cot." Would he relapse, rip me off, cheat on me? Would I end up standing in the Visitors line at County Jail, accepting expensive collect phone calls like the wives and girlfriends.

But there were so many similarities, synergies, symmetries, and passions—(of all kinds). And we worked really well together. There was something very catalytic about our connection, and the momentum of building Beit T'Shuvah experienced a quickening. He was the missing piece.

And we had found each other. When there were millions of reasons for that never to have happened. I see it as part of the miracle and the prayer.

Beshert is the Hebrew word that describes a meant-to-be event of divine guidance, will, and timing. I believed then and I believe now—after more than 20 years—that Mark and I (and God) came together for a purpose to do and be something more than each of us could do alone. We met because we both hit rock bottom and had spiritual clarity and our choices—bad and good—brought us to the moment of intersection. Without our meeting, Beit T'Shuvah would not be what it's become—and a lot of things wouldn't have happened.

Soulmates, yes.

But it ain't always easy.

Mark sums it up: "When I met Harriet, she was suicidal and now she's homicidal."

Ergo, The Morning Parking Lot Test.

I measure the well-being of my marriage in the Beit T'Shuvah parking garage every morning when I arrive at work. Do I feel relief or do I feel irritation at the sight of my husband's car in its space? I haven't kept a chart of the ratio, but I assume I like him more days than not since we've stayed together for over 20 years. When I like him a lot and feel connected, my anxiety about losing him escalates and I worry about plane crashes, car accidents and heart attacks in the middle of the night. When I feel I'd be better off without him, I don't give a shit. Relief or irritation?

It's painful either way.

~

The Jewish tradition defines the role of mate as *Ezer Keneq Do*— one who supports your doing what is right and "grinds against you" when you ain't right. The rules are really simple: If I want you to act from your highest self, I have to act from mine. For instance, if I'm in the supermarket after an argument or when I'm pissed off, I hesitate before selecting the things I know he likes and have to admonish myself before putting them into the cart. Do the next right thing, no matter what you feel.

The mundane truth about marriage/committed relationships is that the same principles of acceptance and challenge show up: accepting both/and's and imperfections requires the same feats of maintenance, housekeeping, and faith as the other things. Bad relationships come naturally, good ones don't.

One of our sages pointed out that if you wait until you have time to study you will never study. There is never time to do the things that require effort and discipline. Taking each other for granted is spending all your relationship currency on everyone but your mate and expecting him/her to understand and to spend it all on you. A marriage requires time and effort if it is to thrive.

In the book, *The Road Less Traveled*, M. Scott Peck describes love as the will to extend oneself for the purpose of nurturing the emotional and spiritual well-being of self and other; helping one another to act from one's highest self for the benefit of self and other.

And that is our mantra—what we try to live by and to teach: Love is not a feeling. Love is acting in loving ways— in spite of what you feel. Both of us go to God for marriage counseling.

~

At Beit T'Shuvah, issues of love and relationships come up on a daily basis—sometimes awe-inspiring, sometimes catastrophic. I share what I have learned and what I'm still learning from reading many books, observing many people and situations, and from my own list of bad relationships and one really, really good one. It basically comes down to some version of this basic riff, a hodge-podge of the principles, policies, and practices we think are important:

Loving is a learned skill. It is a choice and its maintenance requires practice. Its purpose is to grow spiritually and emotionally, separately and together. The basis of spiritual partnership is to stretch each person's capacity to love and forgive.

If I acted badly I can restore myself to wholeness and repair the damage I have done to myself and you through the process of t'shuvah: accepting responsibility, making amends, having a plan and making a commitment not to do it again. Every event or interaction is an opportunity to move toward light or darkness, toward connection or separation, toward love or fear.

A spiritual partnership is a covenantal relationship in which each of us makes a covenant with God and with each other to behave in certain ways. The purpose of the covenant is to help us separate our actions from our desires, impulses and appetites, to take right action no matter what we feel.

Loving relationships (romantic or familial) do not come naturally. Lust comes naturally; romance comes naturally; falling in love comes naturally; anger and jealously come naturally. Often Love is confused with Desire—the best high there is, better than food or drugs in the early stages. Scientists who study the biology of desire have called this feeling limerence. The fusion of sexual excitation and romantic fantasy releases chemicals into the brain equivalent to a speed bath. The feeling of "Falling in love" happens to you, you do not choose it. It lifts you out of your human limitations and flips you to Bliss. You lose your appetite; you don't need sleep; you can do no wrong; you become immortal and your love will never end.

And then it drops you—whether you break up or just stay together long enough. You become a pumpkin again, returned to the ashes of your ordinary mortal, imperfect self. What happened? Where did it go? You come out of the ether and your Prince/Princess has vanished. You try to recapture the high but once you've seen behind the curtain, it's all over. You blame yourself. You blame her or him. You try harder. You leave and find a new one and begin the cycle anew. Or you get disappointed and resentful. It is the same addictive cycle as all other addictions, chasing the first high.

Or you look at one another as real people and commit to a working relationship.

That's what we did.

~

Mark and I were married in a friend's backyard in the Valley by three Rabbis—his, mine and ours—dressed like a gangster and a gun moll. Our covenant (or personal *ketubah*) was a result of both individual and couple spiritual work. It was complicated because I had to learn how to be his wife, after being his boss, his friend and his lover.

When couples come to Rabbi Mark for preparation for marriage he requires them to write individual and couple vows—like we did. The purpose of a *brit*, a covenantal relationship from which there is no escape is to reconnect with God.

He shows them our covenant as a template:

> *I will not use your vulnerabilities against you when I am angry or hurt (no hitting below the belt).*
> *I will be responsible for my own emotional well-being and not expect you to make me happy or share my pain.*
> *I will not punish you with withdrawal of love when I disapprove of you.*
> *I will listen to you even when I disagree with you and consider your point of view.*
> *I will refrain from I-told-you-so's and be gracious no matter which one of us turns out to be 'right.'*
> *I will act lovingly no matter what I think or feel!*
> *I will tell you the truth (at least 90% of the time); we allow each other our secrets.*
> *I won't whine. I will nag when it's for our own good.*
> *I will forgive you your flaws, aware that you are forgiving mine.*
> *I will continue to stretch beyond my limits for the purpose of nurturing my, your and our spiritual and emotional growth.*

Rabbi Twerski admitted at a lecture that sometimes he had to *daven* (pray) for three hours to get thirty seconds with God; those rare moments of connection, free of distraction, resentment, or fear.

In marriage sometimes you have to spend weeks or months acting lovingly even when you don't feel it, to get thirty seconds of soul connection. I try to make it last as long as possible, replaying the moment, smiling to myself, writing about it, telling someone else, reassuring myself that I love him.

Despite the challenges of living and working together, we have honored our marriage and have learned to "manage" our relationship and Beit T'Shuvah at the same time. We complement each other's emotional assets and liabilities. When I don't like him for things he can't change, there's no point telling him about it. Mostly I talk to myself—because almost all our friends and colleagues are part of the Beit T'Shuvah community and I don't want anyone to think badly of him. He's an intense man and creates enough bad feelings all by himself. And I remind myself of Rabbi Omer-Man's lesson that your mate should not be your major source of emotional nurture.

In turn, Beit T'Shuvah has kept our marriage together. Working together has forced us to resolve our differences—neither one of us is willing to risk a divorce and lose "custody" of Beit T'Shuvah. Good management and a loving relationship require the same skill set: again we have to do the next right thing, no matter what we feel. That's impossible to do if feelings dictate actions.

Practice does not make perfect.

There are still days that we can't stand one another and I retreat in sullen silence.

And then Mark will say or do something that shows me how intimately he knows me and I am grateful. We had one of our most intimate moments in the midst of one of those awful days when he heard my unspoken nasty thoughts and spoke them out loud with accuracy and good humor.

Never had I felt so loved and loving or laughed so joyfully.

And as always, the feeling of being felt.

FROM GENERATION TO GENERATION

In the months before my mother Molly's 100th birthday, we began a love affair. Loving one another hasn't come naturally; we had to learn how to do it. Molly girdled her emotions, and mine hung out all over the place. I blamed her for my misery. She waited patiently for me to return.

And I did.

The connection started at a Sarasota Starbucks before her centennial party, and she opened up about our troubled past: "They were bad times, Har... The Depression, the war, your father's gambling. We were all victims of the times." Her next sentence was her greatest gift to me—an understanding of why I am the way I am.

"I always treated you as a person," she said," not as my daughter." That is what made me think she was my enemy.

David Nadell, my father, had a heart attack and died when I was 14. He took the happy part of my heart with him. My life was rocked, and we were on our own.

In my mind while growing up, I was the protagonist in an allegory, Dave and Molly archetypes who pulled on opposite ends of a rope with me tied in the middle. Molly was control, obedience, duty, propriety, containment; Dave was disobedience, spontaneity, authenticity and irreverence. She toilet trained and scheduled me, he bathed and splashed me, played silly games and sang to me. He loved surprises and preached that luxuries were a necessity; she was tight and sensible. He wore his heart out, wearing it on his sleeve; she wore hers in. He died; she lived.

I didn't want to be a separate person. I wanted to be a little girl, her little girl, fused. But Molly prided herself on being objective about me—not making excuses for my bad behavior. I hated that. I wanted her to take my side, approve of everything I wanted (or did) and make a big fuss over me. I wanted surprise birthday parties with balloons, pink-wrapped presents with silver ribbons, and homemade cookies arriving at camp and college.

But for me now, a grown woman, her simple statement unlocked a complicated life-long and painful riddle. It changed how I see myself not only as a daughter, mother, and grandmother—but as a professional.

And it forged a new respect and understanding.

My grandmother was also widowed young, and my mother had to mother her mother, navigating her immigrant family through their new land. Then my father died, and she was left with me and not much else. She refused to fall apart and got on with the business of living. She gave bridge lessons. She played in tournaments and found another husband. She earned independence and resilience and a stiff upper lip in the process. And eventually so did I. The emotions are there and felt deeply—in private.

I experience the chain of connection to the women before me, as strength waiting to be called upon. We have resilience and grit. "Tough broad" is my husband's fondest term of endearment.

When I hear about my mother's days of doctors, deaths, Derby parties and serious bridge, I *kvell* with pride and gratitude to still have her as my role model for aging with grace. No *kvetching* or feeling sorry for herself. The qualities and character that I admire in her as an adult, I despised as a child, especially when we lost my father.

I thought I had to choose between them, and I polarized their positions. Loyalty to Dave's blessed memory (though I never visited his gravesite, said Kaddish or carried his picture in my wallet) required rebellion, but it would have to wait until Molly's daughter finished college, got married and had a baby. But I know that my ability to balance—Molly on the outside and Dave on the inside—kept me away from jails, institutions and death, earned me a Masters degree, a good vocabulary, good manners and the strength of character to sustain myself and eventually carry out my purpose and vision.

It's tempting, sometimes, to play the "what if" game.

What if my father had lived, if by-pass surgery had been available? Would I have come through adolescence with the surety of knowing my beauty reflected in my father's eyes? If I hadn't been an only child, would I have felt less isolated, learned how to get mad and make up? Looking backward, I can see that both my ex's were good husbands. If I had known then when I know now I could have stayed reasonably married to either of them. Would I have settled into the suburban housewife if I hadn't been restless, irritable and discontented?

Were my missteps, sins, and missing the marks all necessary in order to learn how to love and be loved, each false move adding a piece of my puzzle, preparing me to do the work I'm doing now? Or was it leading me, pre-ordained somewhere, a cosmic treatment plan? What about the suffering I caused my ex husbands, my daughter, my mother—part of the process? Is that part of their treatment plan?

I can't answer what if's, and I resist that temptation to try to do so. All I know is that I've landed where I belong, and I'm grateful for all my lessons and all my teachers. Dave's death forced me to grow up and gave me the wisdom to help others do the same.

I think though, he would have loved the woman I have become. I have found what he was searching for. I have also found the man who knows my soul and loves the things about me that I love. I think Dave would've loved that Mark's as irreverent as he was and as loyal, and that he's not cheap or cowardly and he's a good earner and he's fun, and could beat him at rummy or pinochle.

~

I didn't and don't fit into the traditional roles of daughter, mother, and grandmother.

Like many of my clients, I struggle with what is and what I wish had been and done, and what I wish I had given and been given.

And I struggle with the fact that my lackings have caused pain.

And that brings me to my daughter, Delia.

She is a lovely grown up and human—a physician with her own daughters, a maverick and force of change in her own right.

I am sorry to say that I didn't come to the lighter, better parts of myself—spirituality, love of Jewish life, or turning the corner on despair—in time to create a warm and stable home for Delia. I didn't create the kind of orderly life I've come to love, grounded by the weekly blessing of lighting Shabbat candles and prayers over *challah*. And in fact, my moods, dissatisfactions, messiness, and erratic relationships created chaos, rancor and confusion. It affected her.

The sins of the fathers (and mothers) go unto the third and fourth generation. You can't give what you didn't get. I was a 27 year old emotional adolescent when I gave birth to Delia. I loved being pregnant and delivered on the "Natch." But when I had to figure out what she needed and then put her needs before my own, I failed her. I was scared all the time, unable to soothe either of us. The never-ending responsibility of keeping both of us alive made me want to die.

And I finally knew my mother.

I had become her.

Back when I first told Molly I was pregnant, she sighed, "I hope you know what you're doing, Harr; in the end I'm not sure it's worth it." "You mean I wasn't worth it?" Her admission that I had not been a source of joy to her eviscerated me. She was a monster...I'd never do that to my daughter...

But I did.

What went wrong? I wanted Delia. I wanted to be the mother I wanted. I read all the parenting books, bought the right layette, went to natural childbirth classes and joined the La Leche League. I loved nursing and my milk flowed easily.

What I didn't love was the 24-7 responsibility, that she came first, that her needs trumped mine, that I couldn't sleep through the night or read a book or eat a meal without listening for the cry.

My life was no longer mine.

What kind of a monster was I? Why didn't I feel unconditional love? Who could I tell? I looked at the other mothers on the benches in Riverside Park and they appeared blissful. If they were feeling like I was, no one was talking about it. So I kept my feelings a secret and tried to act my part. The only one I couldn't hide from, however, was my child, Delia. She kept tugging at me, needing to be number one. I knew her need—I had been her.

I was ashamed. I was a miserable role-model. Not surprisingly, when she finally became her own person she didn't like me and didn't want to be like me. I recognized the feeling. Dare I say: I treated her too as a "person." And I know it broke her heart. Also, I was a rebel, which she didn't want to be, and my weird behavior embarrassed her. We each realized at some point we would have to save ourselves if we were to survive, and thank God it's turned out to be good for both of us.

I thought everything would get resolved when my daughter had her girls and I became a grandmother.

Wishful thinking.

I went from being a mother who lacked the giddy factor and didn't carry a wallet full of baby pictures, to being a busy, professional grandmother of the same ilk. I felt guilty and angry every time my daughter told me of a grandmother who left wherever she lived and moved to be closer to be with the grandchildren. And I felt bad knowing that Delia probably wanted me to uncover something latent I'd lacked in motherhood, in grandmother-hood. But it didn't happen. I never did become the kind who bakes Christmas cookies with the girls.

But we are finding our ways, making connections, staying true to who we all are.

~

Mark always talks about things being in their proper measure. I understand that being too much of a "person" can be damaging, but I also have come to see that in families, the lack of person-ness and individuation can also be damaging.

One day I ran into somebody I knew casually on a walk in Beverly Hills and offered the usual How are you?

"Can't complain," he replied. "My oldest son is graduating, my daughter is a speech therapist working with stroke victims... If my kids are good, I'm good."

I grew more and more irritated about the interchange for the next 20 blocks.

If my kids are good, I'm good...?

There's always a woman in one of my parent groups who lets me know a mother is only as happy as her unhappiest child: I react every time. This is the hard-ass part of me. I tell her that I believe that each of us bears responsibility for our own well-being. Parental responsibility is circumscribed and time-limited. It is a part of our life cycle as social animals: children become parents who become grandparents. When our children become adults we resume the responsibility for finding fulfillment within ourselves and living our lives with and on purpose.

Most will not say it, but they disagree with me. There is a bias against being fine when your children are not.

As a therapist, I believe it's wrong to place the burden of our well-being on our children. We give them the power to destroy us or redeem us, for which they resent us or try desperately to please us. Either way they are thwarted in their search for their own souls, purpose and truth.

That's why I like the tribal concept.

Dr. Gabor Maté believes that "children were meant to be raised in a tribe, a village, an extended family where the 'wise' elders attune to help raise the young, while the still able-bodied but not yet spiritually and emotionally developed, hunt for food and provide shelter." I love that idea, and believe that's what we've created at Beit T'Shuvah. I've always known that it's the belonging to a community that heals people. It's the real high of soul connection.

The ideal is: "If I'm good, I'm good," and "If they're good, they're good." If I'm having a lousy day, the realization that my daughter is a doctor who is raising two lovely children does not change my reality. My lousy day is my responsibility—not my mother's, not my daughter's, and not my husband's. And if they're having a lousy day, I can still have a good day! It doesn't mean I can't love you—love does not demand that I worry or have to berate myself or you if you are not living according to my plan.

For better and worse, my emotional well-being is not umbilically attached to my daughter's emotional well-being, or her accomplishments or failures. I can't really claim credit or blame for her life choices. I am one of the many influences that have shaped her, particularly the part of her that doesn't want to be anything like me. The part of me that didn't want to be anything like my mother. It's such an old story; it seems to be biblically ordained: in the quest for self we are obligated to shrug off our parents. We don't have to take it personally as parents.

Separation is part of God's plan.

~

My mother's reflections at Starbucks that day about raising me to be a person, led me to a great professional insight. I had an epiphany that made me understand my life—failures, and successes, and see my role as mother and daughter—in a new light.

At the same time, I read *Power Genes* by Maggie Craddock, and a passage about leadership styles described four Power Types. I clearly fit the Inspirer. "Inspirers do not just think outside the box, they frequently ignore the box altogether. They walk their talk, practice what they preach." The author explains the correlation between family background and one's Power Persona: "In an inspirer system, the care-givers tend to define themselves as individuals rather than basing their sense of identity on the role they play in the system." As someone who was treated as a "person," I was able to develop outside the box and that's meant everything to finding my purpose and making it work.

These two events collided in an Oh My God!

I silently reviewed all the messages my mother gave me that I felt as wounds and re-heard them as the truth of myself and life, the permission to become a separate person, not defined by roles or rules: Molly was more person than mother, and of course, so am I. Delia was wounded in the same ways.

And—she too has become an inspirer and visionary, an extraordinary woman who also sees that the Emperor has no clothes on. She stands alone in the middle of medicine, trying to tell everyone that doctors have more questions than answers, that there is no one way for everyone. She's also a missionary, her mission to "heal the heart of medicine."

~

I'm grateful for the blessing of time and good genes, and a peacefulness and acceptance is emerging in my family relationships, as is a coming together of all the parts.

My role as leader of this familial tribe, as CEO, as one who ensures its well being and legacy, is complicated. I conceived it, created it and have maintained it for 25 years, one day-at-a-time. It is the family where I am free to be me without pretense. Where I can fuck-up and not have to give up. A place that demands that I face and walk through a lot of fears with the help of my "posse."

My mother relies on me more as she's becoming less independent. I realize—from generation to generation really matters to me. My mother matters to me profoundly. I treasure our recent email exchange:

> *Dearest Mother Molly,*
> *I think both of us experienced an unusual intimacy during our visit and I want to try to maintain it even from afar. I, too, am feeling the loss but mine is buffered by my full life. It was a great blessing for me to take care of you and love you with action. Not many women my age get to mother their mothers. Our bond is very strong. I don't think either of us bonds easily with others and our friendship is built on years of knowing one another at different stages of our lives. It is irreplaceable and it is not extinguished by distance. Both of us are readers, thinkers and writers.*
> *Our iPads keep us connected.*

I invite a correspondence with you, the kind that friends and lovers have engaged in forever, a sharing of souls. Your immortality resides in me.
I hope this doesn't make you feel worse. I love you dearly.

My Darling,
I have quite long ago begun to feel this strong bond with you. You know me well enough to know how difficult it is for me to express its depth. You know, too, how hard it is to relinquish my independence. It's hard for me to feel so needy, yet those few days we had together were warm and natural. How can I express the anguish of the awareness of how few they must be! My brain knows and accepts but my heart hurts. Am I ready—I wonder. I'm grateful for your productive, happy life with Mark and I can only love you with my whole being.

I am learning to blend my biological family and Mark's biological family with my Beit T'Shuvah family. It's tough stuff, requiring daily maintenance and sacred housekeeping.

My daughter and I are getting closer and respect one another as people. My grandmother moment happened during a family gathering in Palm Springs. Delia mentioned that Marina, the oldest, was becoming a serious shopper. I organized an excursion to the Outlet stores in Banning for the three generations of girls. She's tall and slender and a size 0 and was stunning in everything she put on. I encouraged and indulged her to "go for it."

She told me she was grateful to have a cool, "bling" Baba instead of a cookie-cutter (cookie-making?) one.

My daughter smiled… "You finally got one!"

I forgive myself for being mis-attuned to my daughter. I forgive my mother for being mis-attuned to me.

A HEART OF PEACE

In late January, 2011, things were crazed as always before the yearly Gala. What was different is that Mark and I were the Honorees. I was chosen for being Founder and CEO, and Mark for his role as Rabbi and Spiritual Leader. I felt all the old fears of 'What if I give a party and nobody comes?' Thankfully, people were stepping up with donations.

The Beit T'Shuvah fundraiser is a huge deal philanthropic event in LA, all the Machers in town come to the Beverly Hilton Hotel. This year the dress code was "sparkles." Indeed. Sparkles and bling—my trademark.

As I worked on the acceptance speech that I would give in front of 950 people, it became obvious to me that Beit T'Shuvah, the organization, and Mark and I had grown up together—our personal growth and Beit T'Shuvah's growth, a reflection of one another. And that this was a year of milestones. Married twenty years. Twenty years of Mark's sobriety and ten years since his Rabbinic Ordination. We'd just bought new buildings and we were expanding offices. My book-to-be and speaker series. John Sullivan winning the Social Innovation FastPitch that put us on the map for BTS Communications. Knock Out Addiction fundraiser night. The music program. The family program. The LA Marathon and surf therapy group.

I thought about how we'd matured in our operations as well. We have a branded image and message, a plan of succession, management systems, reliable data collection and base marketing and social media excellence. We produced our first Annual Report, complete with pie-charts! We have a real estate portfolio, no mortgages. From a shack and tent in the back on Lake Street, downtown LA, to four buildings with a value of millions of dollars in west Los Angeles. So many to thank. So many accomplishments, milestones, clients and families we had served. We had become mainstream!

So why—on the day before this big honor—was I staring at my closet, pissed at myself?

Yup. The closet thing.

Again.

Like the cleansing exercise before Bat Mitzvah years before, I focused on things I wanted to leave behind. Harriet, The Honoree, the Founder/CEO of a major non-profit organization—still had a closet that looked like a crazy person's. And what made it worse, and clear evidence of my "addiction," is that I was throwing a silent tantrum as I shoved yet another pair of cool boots into a garbage bag, awaiting donation.

This time, it wasn't hidden though. It wasn't fraudulent or secret.

My daughter, The Doctor, (with perfect closet habits), was sternly holding up items like a fashion segment of "This is Your Life:" camouflage era, cowboy boot obsession, Hawaiian…

"When was the last time you wore this…?" She demanded, as she lifted a sequined wrap from the pile. The Indian Skirt phase— long forgotten in favor of my most recent style incarnation: chic business suits plus just-enough bling.

"But it might be vintage someday."

It was in the bag before the words came out.

The irony was clear: I was being acknowledged for my life's work dealing with the bad habits of others, and there I was, dealing with the same old, same old problems, and like any addict, staring longingly at 25 giant lawn & leaf bags of giveaway shoes, purses, jeans and other stuff, still leaving a full closet, albeit, somewhat neater.

"And why do you need 30 pairs of jeans…?"

Even I knew there was no good answer. My closets suggested the obsessive-compulsive Hoarders segment rather than Martha Stewart.

But in spite of my imperfections, I was at it again. And I would my whole life—my way of choosing life, making effort. And I knew then that the following night, as I read my speech, Harriet Honoree/Harriet Hoarder would stand side by side, at peace, together at last!

～

Although I've had the Chief Executive Officer title for just over a decade, it's only in the last few years that I feel entitled to it. For a long time I felt like a fraud because I couldn't read the balance sheet and the budget meetings bored me. But now Beit T'Shuvah has become a mature, mainstream organization, capable of sustainability, scalability and succession planning. I have become a mature woman capable of sustaining my vision and maintaining relationships. I love my work and I work with my love.

Early on, I wasn't a great manager (and still have to work on it), and I didn't know how to negotiate the personal and the professional title. I liked some of my employees (those who liked and agreed with me) and ignored the ones who didn't like me or made me question myself. Although I didn't intend it, I fostered a culture of allies and enemies.

I had to learn to apply our basic principles like 'do the next right thing no matter what you feel,' and 'become more a God pleaser than a People pleaser'. I had to be willing to not be liked and to make unpopular decisions. I had to increase my tolerance for ambiguity and uncertainty. To allow conflict and handle it gracefully. This hasn't been easy for me. I have enemies. Some of the people I've helped want to hurt me when they hurt themselves and blame Beit T'Shuvah for their failures.

Beit T'Shuvah is a reflection of my longing for love and acceptance. In a way, it's the family I wished I had had and the family I wish I'd created in my home with Delia. It's the community that wants me as a member, a place where I belong. I am matriarch, Rebbetzin, woman of wisdom with all my eccentricities and irregularities. The good thing is that I have had a chance to become the type of mother I wished for and, to the residents, I am the mother they wished they had had. I accept them with all their eccentricities, idiosyncrasies and felonies. I expose my imperfections and life struggles. My successes and failures. I accept fuck-ups as part of success.

The staff finally persuaded me to offer a series of talks we titled: "Harriet Dishes the Dirt." I sat on a stool on the bima, made eye contact with a packed room and opened my mouth. No props. Only a microphone, a black stool and a coffee mug that read: "Shalom Motherfucker." For years and years my only audience had been a bunch of recovering addicts in my various workshops during the day, and my staff, who had to listen to me. But this was different. They could get up and leave, but didn't. Many of them were therapists, used to Power Point seminars. My style was more personal than professional and I was scared of their disapproval. But they loved me. Thank you for being so honest! My secrets were their secrets, too!

A good CEO is a person of "passionate curiosity," according to Adam Bryant in his book *The Corner Office*. He walks his talk. He/She trickles down authentic, transparent and imperfect without retribution. She/He makes it right to be wrong and to see that consequence is not punishment. Personal growth is given a higher value than proficiency or perfection. And lo and behold, cooperation fosters more creativity than competitiveness. No one has to be wrong for me to feel right.

I still want to leave town when I have to fire someone and live in terror of their vengeance and litigiousness. I still want everyone to like me and have said yes when I should have said no, so people wouldn't be mad at me. Once or twice recently I endangered the organization by not saying no and not firing an employee.

I'm getting better at it. I've learned to protect me from myself by choosing advisors who are willing to tell me the truth in a way that I can hear it.

Mark and I have grown individually and as a partnership in our struggle to tell each other the truth and to hear it without defending or striking back. The worst times were when I would "fall in love" with a new guru or savior and Mark would smell bullshit. I was never sure if he was right or just jealous. Often I would get mad at Mark and strengthen my alliance with the other person to the detriment of all of us and Beit T'Shuvah. Mark has been right enough times that I listen to him when his bullshit detector lights up. He is also his most gracious and generous when he is right, resisting "I told you so" and even saying he's sorry to be right.

My other advisors have been able to show me the way to sustain Beit T'Shuvah without sacrificing my vision or squelching my rebel spirit. They have helped build the management systems necessary for succession and sustainability and to brand and market our message through social media to increase visibility and generate friends and funds.

My job as "Boss" is to role model a "heart of peace" even when I have to correct you or terminate your employment. I have to manage my own emotions, see everyone for who they are not who I want them to be, not take their mistakes or inadequacies personally, find the place where they can shine and reflect their light back to them.

I don't have to know how to do the financials but I do have to know how to manage the CFO and encourage the financial office to become part of the team. I don't have to know how to ask a donor for a major gift; I do have to cultivate relationships, know how to present and package our message and how to contain their hurts, jealousies and fears so they can work cooperatively.

I don't have to know how to do a Power Point presentation. I'm a good enough speaker to tell people what I know from direct experience. I don't need a statistical study to tell me if something works. I can see it. The best scientific studies can be replicated and repeated. Nonetheless, I bow to the need donors and funders have for evidence-based results and best practices formulas. Our partnership with UCLA Department of Addictive Psychiatry is providing the research and credibility we need. Most days I'm too involved in the daily dramas to fully experience the miracle of transformation or to acknowledge myself for helping to change so many lives.

I honor myself for sustaining my vision and maintaining my integrity, most of the time. Science now affirms our integrative, mind/body/spirit approach to treatment, the approach big guys laughed at and dismissed 25 years ago: *a willy-nilly approach... anecdotal evidence has no validity... unprofessional. Ha ha.*

My most significant accomplishment, in my mind, is honoring mission over money and still managing to be fiscally responsible. No one has ever been denied help because they couldn't pay. My lowest moments are when those same people, if they're in trouble or don't get what they want, accuse me and Beit T'Shuvah of giving preferential treatment to the people who pay. If they only knew the tightrope I have to walk to keep this place running. Those moral dilemmas go back to our earliest days.

The mission I have accepted mandates that I become an acrobat, continually balancing the needs of the individual, the small Beit T'Shuvah community and the larger community of donor-consumers.

My efforts will always be imperfect and impure, a sacred blend of holy and profane. Integrity, by definition, must be an integration of conflicting inclinations resulting in a covenant with all of oneself to do the next right thing as you understand it in the moment. I will learn my line in the sand; the place I cannot cross without damaging my soul. Thank God I have Mark and his personal understanding of textual Judaism to guide us. I trust the wisdom of Judaism to guard my integrity, keeping it porous and planted.

I have recovered my passion and discovered my purpose. I have been able to sustain my vision, to walk through fear and self-doubt, to do the next right thing even when I don't want to. Most of the time I walk my talk. When I screw up I'm able to say 'oops!' and learn from my mistakes, not be defeated by them.

～

After 20 years, I am cognizant of how much we've accomplished. I don't feel like the kid who didn't get picked for kick ball. I am comfortable as CEO and leader. I do what needs to be done. We were the honorees and it was a good business decision. I was very relieved that people stepped up, that there's more money so that we can help those who need help for another year. It's part of my job. People say: You've earned it. You deserve it. And, I say—it's a good business decision.

And it was a successful, beautiful night. I spoke…

> *Beit T'Shuvah and I are honored to receive the 2011 T'Shuvah Award. We have been together for 25 years, longer than Mark and I have been married. We have grown up together… You are the people who have guided and supported us in our journey from rebellious adolescent fighting for identity and independence to a mature, sustainable organization that has taken its proper place in the mainstream. Our operations costs have grown from $50,000 to $8-plus million, our staff from one (me) to about 50, plus volunteers, the people we serve from three when the doors opened to over 300 with our outpatient, prevention and community outreach programs. I kvell that 80% of our paid staff are graduates of Beit T'Shuvah…*

Later on, Mark and I sat at our table and held hands like we had so many other times, watching a parade of Alum, coming down the aisles from all parts of the room, onto the stage, saying their name and years of sobriety. Hundreds of real people (not statistics) crowded on the stage, all living sane and sober lives, resurrected. The audience stood and clapped and cheered.

When T'Shuvah works and redemption happens and is maintained and sustained—it's astonishing, thrills people and makes them cry, makes them want to give.

～

My story and the story of the miracle and Beit T'Shuvah is incomplete without addressing the hardest question: what about when it doesn't work?

The belief that transformation is possible is intrinsic to the tenets of Beit T'Shuvah.

And no one knows more than I do how intrinsically flawed and imperfect a process it is.

It's wrought with landmines—bad faith, disappointment, loss, lies, relapse. I have seen people make choices that led to death or prison. I have seen that sometimes it is easier for people to give up drugs than to give up their sense of entitlement. The reality is that when it doesn't work, it can—in our line of work—be really bad, really personal, and the stakes are high. And when our particular brand of rehab fails, it fails big.

Our clients often see me as an elder, an authority with parental powers, an exemplar of rectitude and perfection, exempt from pain and struggle. They deify me when I live up to their expectations and demonize me when I disappoint them. They demand of me what they demand of their parents, that I judge them by their intentions and overlook their actions, but feel entitled to do the opposite with the "grownups."

Many addicts feel judged and victimized and therefore exempt from responsibility and rules. They create scenarios that give them permission to escape. I am hands-on. I demand that they view me as a human, perfectly imperfect just like them and that they take responsibility for their choices. And that's not always pretty. And because dealing in our business is complicated and imperfect—and not just because of the clients and process— some days can be really tough.

I recently came the closest I've ever come to quitting and giving up in over twenty years of daily battle with the demons within and the nay-sayers without.

I was overwhelmed. Increasing numbers of people were demanding equal or greater shares of my attention. A sea of hurt feelings was lapping at my feet, insisting that I look down instead of up: supervisory Training Boards, workman's comp laws, wrongful-termination terrorists, insulted Board members whose names were misspelled or left out threatening to withdraw their support. It felt like "Angry Birds" pecking away at me.

It felt like whoever was giving us money was always threatening to take it away, whether it's insurance companies, the government, paying customers or private donors. It's a kind of servitude. I dance, they pull the strings.

The people who attack from below threaten to withdraw their love and loyalty and to attack your reputation which ultimately costs money in lawsuits or withdrawal of friends. Trusted employees embezzle; they leave for jobs that pay more.

And sometimes, the day-to-day complaints and problems threaten my visionary soaring spirit: *His name plaque is shinier than mine... You sat me at a terrible table...* ridiculous requirements for meaningless statistics, bureaucrats with clipboards from every department "investigating" bogus complaints, roommate squabbles, staff jealousies and sibling rivalries, bed bugs, termites, irate neighbors, parking problems, volunteer therapists having tantrums over office space and requiring me to soothe them so they can soothe the clients. Some days I think of "The Little Red Hen" who couldn't find anyone to help her bake the bread and then they all showed up to eat it when it was ready.

I'd had it.

I stared at the various emails, phone and text messages, the 911's and the fires I had to put out. I thought to myself: Who, in God's name, will soothe me when I run out of self-soothing tricks?

Mark is a warrior—his demons are fierce and he "wrestles" with them out loud. Very loud, sometimes! He is an exemplar of spiritual imperfection, demanding of himself and everyone else that they fight to defeat the demon we all have that tells us we are not worthy of God's love. He charges into people's defenses and yanks off their masks, screaming that "You Matter!" "Hold On." Sometimes he scares me and I shrivel back to the safety of my inner igloo. "I'm tired of wrestling; turn down the noise; leave me alone." I count on Mark to charge in after me and he counts on me to stop him from driving off the cliff.

And this one day, when Mark became part of the problem, I hit the wall. He stood at my door shouting, "Your stupid staff: no one consults me about a client; never can find them when you need them..."

I couldn't wait for him to leave the building for his lunch date. I don't want to repeat what I thought when I saw his car in its spot.

And then it took him 15 minutes to get out of the garage because "these self-centered, ungrateful bastards we pay don't give a fuck where they park... I'll fire all of them; I surrender; I'll park on the street."

I texted Mark and told him I was no longer capable of fixing everything that was wrong with the world. I picked up my bag and went home to bed. I scared the shit out of him and I was glad. I meant to.

I slept it off, was back at my desk early the next morning.

Another day.

Another chance.

I am spurred on by my own addiction to redemption—in spite of how imperfect it is. It's my drug of choice.

I know from experience that if I just "hold on," I'll get to witness another thrilling miracle of transformation. I'll listen to Cantor Rachel singing the *Kedusha* on Friday night in the company of her angels and remember how she came to Beit T'Shuvah having "lost her voice" and wanting to die. Thank You, God, for helping me breathe life into her soul (and lungs). I'll get to share the excitement of our John Sullivan winning the Social InnovationFast Pitch award at the USC School of Business.

These are the big payoffs, the major miracles, the obvious ones.

But there are thousands and thousands and thousands of other tiny, cool moments that are grounded in the everyday miracles:

a man who has never held a legitimate job comes home waving his first paycheck; a young girl boasts that she hasn't thrown up for a whole week, the longest period she's had since she was fourteen. I get to be the "other mother" of the bride at the few Beit T'Shuvah weddings we have every year, and to kvell when they want to bring their children "home" for Shabbos. I love being a matchmaker and a grandmother to the next generation of sober, spiritually evolving human beings who might never have been if not for Beit T'Shuvah.

I think back to my short meeting with the "expect a miracle" lady Janet Levy decades before.

"Father of the Universe, take this woman by the hand and guide her to her rightful work. She knows she has a mission but she doesn't know what it is."

"That's it?"

"That's it for now. You just pay attention."

I am still paying attention.

There are always those in need of help.

And I am grateful. The unexpected, unlikely miracle is still unfolding.

THE END

~

AFTERWORD

Completing this book is major miracle, a monumental feat of Sacred Housekeeping. The perfect "House Keeper" (editor) collected, sorted and organized over twenty years of handwritten legal pads and shaped them into this book. It was a holy collaboration… Reeva, me and God. I would have quit without them.

And now I have to release the results. If one person has an "Aha" that helps them live more authentically, I have accomplished my mission. Would I love it to make the best seller list of the *New York Times Book Review*? You bet! Either way I win!

I am available to speak to whoever wants to listen.

ABOUT THE AUTHOR

Harriet Rossetto is the CEO and Founder of Los Angeles's renowned non-profit drug and alcohol treatment organization, Beit T'Shuvah. Harriet received her Masters in Social Work from the University of Minnesota in 1964 and is a much sought-after speaker in synagogues and community groups as well as a trainer for the National Association of Social Workers. Harriet lives in Los Angeles with her husband, Rabbi Mark Borovitz.